MW01290510

Create

A Biblical Guide to Becoming

the Woman God Designed You

to Be

AMY DUGGINS

Contents

Introduction

I'm so grateful you have joined me on this journey towards becoming the women we were created to be! If you are reading these words, I don't believe it is by accident. I believe God has specifically placed this book in your life so you may know Him better, grow spiritually, and reflect His goodness to everyone around you. His desire is for you to live in close relationship with Him, a relationship marked by faith, trust, and obedience. He longs for you to be a woman who steps into becoming everything He designed you to be. God created you on purpose and for a purpose!

The best way we can get to know God is by studying the Bible. Whether you are a seasoned Bible reader or have never opened a Bible in your life, God's will for you is to know and comprehend His Word. Please don't feel intimidated or worry about not being able to understand the Bible. There are many easy-to-read translations and God will always provide wisdom and understanding to His passages. He wrote the Bible, and He wants us to understand it! In the Bible we find the answers to all of life's questions. Who are we and why are we here? How can we live a life of joy and purpose? And most importantly; who is God, and how does He relate to His people? What is His will for my life?

As we read the Bible we will uncover the timeless truths it contains. As we diligently apply those truths to our lives, miraculous transformation will result. The Bible is a beautiful gift from Creator to creation. It is our manual for life, God-breathed and Holy Spirit inspired. It was dictated to different authors, in different countries, in different languages, over a period of 1500 years, yet remains one congruent story of God's redemption and faithfulness. It is historically established and experience confirmed. There is no greater authority than the Word of God. It is unchanging and will endure forever.

This guide to becoming the woman God created you to be was meant to be taken a little at a time. Read a chapter a day, or every few days. Take as long as you feel is necessary to meditate upon each topic. Wherever you are at in your spiritual journey, I am confident the Lord will grow your faith and deepen your understanding through this process.

I encourage you to look up the Scriptures in your own Bible as well. The Old Testament was originally written in Hebrew, and the New Testament in Greek. Many of the chapters in this book contain the definitions for specific words pulled from the original language. Pulling from the original words enriches their meaning and helps to clarify God's intent. Please take the time to allow God's truths to speak to you. Meditate on the Scriptures and thoughtfully reflect upon the questions. Pray the prayers. Ask God for His wisdom on how to specifically apply the information to your life.

Ask God to reveal any misconceptions you may have about Him or His Word. Ask Him to correct any wrong thinking you may have. Ask for forgiveness when necessary. He will be there to lead and grow you. He is full of grace and love, ready to forgive, redeem, and restore. Although sometimes His Word may feel offensive, His purpose is never to condemn you. His intention is to bring about conviction that leads to change. This will guide you into the truth that will result in a transformed life; to His glory, and to your benefit. Allow Him to work on your heart, and draw you ever closer to Him. Allow the Bible to do what God intended for it to do, speak to your soul and align you with His will for your life. There is no greater peace, and no greater joy than intimacy with your Creator, and a life lived inside His perfect will, for this is why you were created!

All Scripture is breathed out by God and profitable for teaching, for reproof, for correction, and for training in righteousness, that the man of God may be complete, equipped for every good work. 2 Timothy 3:16-17 ESV

"You are my witnesses," declares the Lord, "and my servant whom I have chosen, that you may know and believe me and understand that I am He. Before me no god was formed, nor shall there be any after me." Isaiah 43:10 ESV

You will seek me and find me, when you seek me with all your heart. Jeremiah 29:13 ESV

Chapter 1
Created to Follow Jesus

*"If anyone serves me, he must follow me; and where I am,
there will my servant be also. If anyone serves me, the Father
will honor him." John 12:26 ESV*

Follow – *akoloutheo* {Greek} – "To be or become the disciple of
anyone as to faith and practice, to follow his teaching. To
follow closely and intently."

The first step on our journey towards becoming the
women God created us to be is the foundation upon
which every other truth in this book will stand.
Everything else we discuss will flow from this. It begins with a
question: "Am I a disciple of Jesus Christ?" Living as a disciple
of Christ means He is not just the Savior of our souls, He is
Lord over every aspect of our lives. He is given ultimate
authority over our destiny and our will is surrendered to His.
We follow Christ and experience the many blessings He has
for us. We follow Him into freedom and victory. We follow
Him down beautiful paths and beside still waters.

Yet we also follow Him into the difficult places. We follow
Him when it is hard. We stretch and we sacrifice; we yield our
own agenda to His. Following Christ is not always easy or
popular, but it is always worth it. This is God's will for every
single woman on this earth. First, that we are reconciled to
Him by the blood of Jesus. Secondly, that we embark on a
lifelong journey of following Jesus' teachings and becoming
more like Him.

Then Jesus told his disciples, "If anyone would come after me, let him deny himself and take up his cross and follow me. For whoever would save his life will lose it, but whoever loses his life for my sake will find it. For what will it profit a man if he gains the whole world and forfeits his soul?"
Matthew 16:24-26a ESV

In a world that claims there are many roads to God; the Bible's truth still stands. Jesus is the only way. He is the way, the truth, and the light. No-one comes to the Father except through Him. Therefore, our first step in becoming the women God created us to be is to ensure we have trusted in Jesus for our salvation. Are we believing and trusting in Christ and Christ alone to save our souls? The Greek word for believe is *pisteuo*, which means to entrust one's spiritual well-being to Christ. In order to entrust our spiritual well being to Him, we must know why it is so necessary.

The saying is trustworthy and deserving of full acceptance, that Christ Jesus came into the world to save sinners, of whom I am the foremost. 1 Timothy 1:15 ESV

For God so loved the world that He gave His only Son, that whoever believes in Him should not perish but have eternal life. John 3:16 ESV

Contrary to popular belief, no human being will ever be good enough to enter heaven based on his or her own merit. Our best efforts at being a good person are horribly inadequate when held up to the light of a Holy God. You might be a really nice person who is kind to others and who does a lot of good deeds. You may even have an impressive list of "churchy" activities on your resume. Unfortunately, good as those deeds might be, they are just not good enough.

We, as a human race, are inherently sinful. Sin is forever embedded into our DNA, passed down from Adam and Eve's decision in the garden to eat fruit from the forbidden tree. None of us could ever live up to God's expectations in our own strength. He is Holy. He knows all, sees all, and discerns every hidden thought and motive. Every one of us has missed the mark; even on our best day we are still too sinful. We need a Savior, someone to please God on our behalf. Someone who's perfect obedience can take the place of all of our imperfections.

For all have sinned and fall short of the glory of God.
Romans 3:23 ESV

For our sake He made Him to be sin who knew no sin, so that
in Him we might become the righteousness of God.
1 Corinthians 5:21 ESV

Because God is Holy and holds us to righteous standards, when a sin is committed there must be a sacrifice to cover that sin. Blood is required to atone for the transgression so that we might again be able to stand in God's holy presence. Without blood, there is no reconciliation, no peace with God. The blood of animals sufficed to cover sins in the Old Testament but it could never take away sins to the extent that the sinner would be truly pure. Sacrifices had to be offered again and again, because the blood of animals could never fully remove sins.

But in these sacrifices there is a reminder of sins every year.
For it is impossible for the blood of bulls and goats to take
away sins. Hebrews 10:3-4 ESV

All along, God had a better plan. A new covenant. One death for sins: once and for all. This death would not only atone for every sin, but it would also impart permanent reconciliation with God. It would provide freedom from sin and victory over Satan, the enemy of our souls. This sacrifice would perfect us from the inside as we drew near to God in faith. Purify us and wash us clean. Our Heavenly Father loves us so much that He sent His son Jesus, a piece of Himself, to suffer and die on a cross. Jesus endured the punishment we deserve. He died a sinner's death and then in three days He rose again to complete God's incredible plan of redemption.

This is the amazing grace of God! Jesus suffered and paid the debt we owed so we could be free. While we were still sinners God sent Jesus to die so that we may have eternal life through Him. Now, because of this, we are seen as righteous. When God looks at us He doesn't see all of our imperfections, He sees the perfect obedience of Christ. We have been removed from darkness and transferred to the kingdom of God's glorious light. We are now a part of God's family. We are His children, precious and dearly loved.

But to all who receive Him, who believed in His name, He gave the right to become children of God. John 1:12 ESV

This salvation is available to everyone, yet exclusive at the same time. Peace with God and eternal life in heaven can be obtained by every single person in this world. Regardless of nationality, social status, or religion. Regardless of where we have been or what we have done. God does not show partiality.

He offers salvation to anyone who repents (shows pious sorrow for unbelief and sin) and turns to Jesus. Anyone who makes the decision to entrust their spiritual well-being to Christ. That's where it gets exclusive. We must respond to this invitation of eternal life with God. We must respond with our minds *and* our hearts. It is not just intellectual assent to what Jesus has done for us. It is true belief. To believe is to follow.

Following Jesus means He is not only our Savior, He is also our Lord.

> *Blessed are those whose lawless deeds are forgiven, and whose sins are covered; blessed is the man against whom the Lord will not count his sin. Romans 4:7-8 ESV*

Once we truly understand the gravity of our situation and the tremendous gift Jesus has given us, there is no other way to respond besides following Him. We must turn from our old ways of trusting in ourselves and instead put Jesus in charge. When we make the decision to repent, place faith in Jesus, and turn to God with our whole hearts, He sees us differently. Instead of looking at us and seeing our sins, He looks at us and sees the perfect obedience of Christ. Our sins are washed away and we can approach God with confidence, having full confidence that we are a part of His family.

As we seek Him, follow Him, and surrender our will to His, we will grow in maturity. His grace will empower us to be obedient to His commands and our lives will start to transform as we walk in freedom and victory. His love will begin to flow outward to everyone around us as His Holy Spirit takes up residence inside us. We will have a new heart, new desires, and a new mission. A brand new life.

> *Therefore, if anyone is in Christ, he is a new creation. The old has passed away; behold, the new has come.*
> *2 Corinthians 6:17 ESV*

Aren't you glad you don't have to strive to be good enough to earn God's love? I know I am. I came from a childhood where I never felt good enough. I always believed my performance determined my parents' love for me. I'm so grateful I don't have to worry about whether or not I'm performing well enough for God to love me. I don't have to wonder whether my good deeds will be enough to get me into heaven. Once I placed my faith in Jesus Christ, the deal was sealed. I received God's Spirit, which now lives inside me as a guarantee of God's love and my future inheritance.

Now it is God who makes both us and you stand firm in Christ. He anointed us, set his seal of ownership on us, and put His Spirit in our hearts as a deposit, guaranteeing what is to come. 2 Corinthians 1:21-22 NIV

The best part is you don't have to clean yourself up before you come to Jesus. He only requires a humble heart, an open mind, and a willingness to follow where He leads. To become His follower, you need not be a Bible scholar or born into a Christian family. He invites anyone, anywhere, at any time, to follow Him! He often chooses the ones we would least expect. This has been a pattern of His since choosing His very first disciples.

While walking by the Sea of Galilee, he saw two brothers, Simon (who is called Peter) and Andrew his brother, casting a net into the sea, for they were fishermen. And he said to them, "Follow me, and I will make you fishers of men." Matthew 4:18-19 ESV

Jesus could have chosen His followers from any number of the religious elite. He could've selected prestigious, well-respected men to be His disciples. Yet, this wasn't the case. The first men Jesus asked to follow Him were not religious leaders, Scripture teachers or anyone of high importance. They were simple, common men. They worked hard year-round in the heat and the cold. They caught fish and mended nets with their calloused hands. I imagine the smell of fish followed them wherever they went. Jesus didn't inquire about their credentials before He invited the men to follow Him; He chose them because He knew *He* would be the one to equip them for their calling. Throughout the New Testament, we see how Jesus grew the disciples' faith, strengthened their characters, and transformed their lives for His glory. And He continues to do the same for His followers today. It all starts with a simple yes that changes everything. "Yes Jesus, I will follow you."

Trusting in Christ is a beautiful beginning, the start of a brand new relationship, and peace with your Creator. This is what you were created for, what your soul longs for. Peace and intimacy with God. Come as you are, and He will grow a mustard seed of faith into one that will move mountains. Become His disciple and find rest, true rest for your soul.

{At that time Jesus declared} "Come to me all who labor and are heavy laden, and I will give you rest. Take my yoke upon you, and learn from me, for I am gentle and lowly in heart, and you will find rest for your souls. For my yoke is easy, and my burden is light." Matthew 11:28-30 ESV

Personal Reflection:

Have I trusted in Christ for my salvation? Have I acknowledged in my heart and confessed with my lips that Jesus is Lord? Do I believe that He died and rose again as payment for my sins? If the answer is no, confess these things now to the Lord in a humble and heartfelt prayer of repentance.

Am I not only a believer but an actual follower of Jesus? Do I take the time to cultivate my relationship with Him, study His Word, and live out His teachings?

Would I consider myself to be a disciple of Christ? If I feel that I have been more of a Christian in name only, what steps can I take to live out my faith as I actively pursue what it means to be a Christ-follower?

Heavenly Father, we approach You today with humble and grateful hearts. We are so thankful You have made a way for us to have peace with You. Thank you for providing freedom from our sins. We are so grateful that we don't ever have to be "good enough" because Jesus has already pleased You on our behalf. Words cannot express the gratitude we have at His sacrifice. Thank You Jesus for living a sinless life and dying the most brutal death... for us. We can never repay You, yet we hope to live lives that honor and glorify You. It is the least we can do. Help us to believe and trust You in all things. Help us to stay on the right path, following You wherever You lead. Create in us a passion for You, and let nothing and no one stand in the way of our pursuit. We pray also for those who have never made the commitment to following Christ before. We know You receive them with open arms, and this is the beginning of a brand new relationship and a new life for them. Thank You for Your love and Your forgiveness. Thank You for accepting us as we are, but not leaving us that way. Help us to seek You with all of our hearts, for Your Word says we will find You when we seek You with all of our hearts. May this be the beginning of a beautiful journey together into becoming the women You created us to be. May Your praise ever be on our lips. In Jesus beautiful name we pray, Amen.

Chapter 2

Created to Revere God

Older women likewise are to be reverent in behavior.
Titus 2:3 ESV

Reverent: "Feeling or showing deep and solemn respect."
(Devout)

We were created to live in such a way that our deep admiration for Jesus would shine out of all that we do. The Greek Word for reverent is *hieroprepes,* which pertains to being fit or appropriate for a sacred place or person. Specifically in this Scripture this word implies that women are to adorn their profession of Christ with their behavior. The word used for behavior is *katastema,* which suggests external action issuing from the inner life, the heart life. Together, these words refer to godly conduct that is clearly seen in words and actions, flowing from a heart that desires to please God and do His will.

I just love this picture of surrender and obedience pouring out from an inner heart life that adores Jesus and honors His Word. Our behavior starts in our hearts. Our heart life produces our thoughts, which lead to our words and actions (behavior). Therefore, our first step towards being women who are reverent in our behavior is to cultivate a deep love for Jesus in our hearts.

To illustrate this, let's look at the story of Zacchaeus. Zacchaeus was a chief tax collector who lived during the time Jesus walked the Earth. In that day, tax collectors were shunned and looked down upon by the rest of society. This was largely because they cheated people by collecting more tax than what was required, and padded their own pockets with the extra. Tax collectors were notorious sinners, yet these were just the type of people Jesus came to save.

One day Zacchaeus, desperate to get a glimpse of Jesus as He walked by, climbed up a tree to get a better view. As Jesus passed by He noticed Zacchaeus above and requested to stay at Zacchaeus' house. The tax collector climbed down immediately and joyfully greeted Jesus. After welcoming Jesus into his home, Zacchaeus declared that he would give half his goods to the poor and pay back every single person he had cheated four-fold!

The beauty of this story is that Zacchaeus wasn't forced or even *asked* to right his wrongs. Simply being in the presence of Jesus was enough to compel him to do the right thing. Being with Jesus changed this sinful man's heart. He was transformed by the gospel, just like we will be when we commit to putting God first. As we are transformed, reverent behavior will come naturally.

This transformation process involves getting to know Him through the Scriptures and setting aside time to pray and be in His presence. We want to be women who can say, "My heart belongs to Jesus". This is such an important truth to get deep down into our souls as we journey together into becoming the women we were designed to be. Much of what we will discuss in this book will pertain to our actions, and steps we can take to align those actions and our lives with God's standards.

However, behavior modification without real heart change completely misses the point. This will only lead to frustration and place the focus on our achievements and failures, rather than on Jesus where it belongs. When we love God more than anything else, everything falls into place.

And he said to him, "You shall love the Lord your God with all your heart and with all your soul and with all your mind."
Matthew 22:37 ESV

God wants our hearts. From the beginning of Scripture until the end, this is a common theme. He deeply desires relationship with us and He longs for intimacy, as a Father to His children. As we get to know Him (through His Word, prayer, and worship), a true love for Him will begin to blossom in our hearts and overflow into our thoughts and actions. Our desire will be to be obedient to Him in all ways and to please Him.

Living out this reverent behavior means that as women who profess Christ with our lips, we should never deny Him with our lifestyles. Our faith should not be simply what we believe; it should be lived out with every fiber of our being. Our love and respect for the Lord should shine out of us in our words and actions. Others should look to us and think that we are different. We were not created to blend in, but to shimmer and sparkle with the goodness of God wherever we go. Set apart. Different. Holy.

But you are a chosen people, a royal priesthood, a holy nation, God's special possession, that you may declare the praises of Him who called you out of darkness into his wonderful light. 1 Peter 2:9 ESV

God calls us to reverent behavior. He calls us to holy living. Thankfully, we do not have to attempt this in our own strength, because quite frankly, we are not holy by nature. Try to be holy on your own and you will quickly realize (as I did) that your sinful nature will try to creep in and take over every chance it gets. The struggle is real. So real in fact, that Paul spoke of his own struggle when addressing the Roman believers.

For I do not understand my own actions. For I do not do what I want, but I do the very thing that I hate. Now if I do what I do not want, I agree with the law, that it is good. So now, it is no longer I who do it, but sin that dwells within me. For I know that nothing good dwells in me, that is, in my flesh. For I have the desire to do what is right, but not the ability to carry it out. Romans 7:15-18 ESV

It is comforting to know that Paul, the (divinely inspired) writer of half of the New Testament, wrestled with the very same things we do. He desired to live holy, up to God's standards, but did not have the ability to carry it out. We desire to be reverent in our behavior, but we also do not have the ability to carry it out. This is where God's grace enters in. Not only does His amazing grace save us and cover all of our sin, it empowers us to live righteously and obediently.

His divine power has given us everything we need for a godly life through our knowledge of Him who called us by His own glory and goodness. 2 Peter 1:3 NIV

As we pursue Jesus, giving Him our whole hearts, not just a piece of them, we will be sanctified (made holy) by the Holy Spirit. As we read Scripture and work towards living the way God desires, we will discover our areas of weakness. When we surrender these shortcomings to the Lord, we will begin to see His grace at work, and His power shine out of us. When we are weak, we are strong with His strength. As we allow His Word to shape our thoughts and dictate our words and actions, our behavior will change. Throughout this process we will begin to fall in love with God's character. His goodness, His mercy, His compassion, His Holiness. The by-product of this love is a reverence for Him that will be evident to all.

As our relationship with God deepens, our respect for Him will manifest in our actions. We express this respect in our general conduct, but there are also two specific ways we can show our reverence for Him. One way is in how we approach His house, the church. God cares deeply about His church. Church is a place where believers gather together to worship Him, learn His word, and accomplish His will. A healthy, Bible-based, Spirit-filled church will be filled with God's glorious presence. This presence should always be approached in a reverent manner, with humility and awe.

Church is the place we go to worship God. When we enter His sanctuary our focus should be on Him. We put away our phones and we set distracting thoughts to the side. We save our conversations until service is over. This is the time to show our respect for God and gratitude for all He has done for us. It is the time to worship and to open our ears and hearts to hear God's voice. We should always enter His house with an attitude of respect: in our attire, in our attitude, and in our actions. Let us remember we are worshiping the Lord of Lords and the King of Kings!

Praise the Lord! Praise God in His sanctuary; praise him in His mighty heavens! Praise Him for His mighty deeds; praise Him according to His excellent greatness! Psalm 150:1-2 ESV

The second way we reveal our esteem for the Lord is in how we use His name. The name of Jesus is holy. It is the name above all names, and there is great power in speaking it. The name of Jesus should be exalted and magnified. Yet so often we hear His name tossed around frivolously. People use the Lord's name to express disbelief, excitement, frustration, even anger. His name is used in a cursing, derogatory manner. Oh how this must hurt His heart! As followers of Jesus, let the way we use God's name always reflect our respect and honor for Him. His name should be precious to our lips. It should never be used in a careless manner.

You shall not take the name of the Lord your God in vain, for the Lord will not hold him guiltless who takes his name in vain. Exodus 20:7 ESV

I understand this may be a struggle for some. Old habits die hard, especially for those who are just beginning to walk with Christ. The first step is acknowledging where we have gone wrong and asking for forgiveness. When we repent and ask for God's help, we begin the process of change. I misused the name of God many, many times before I made the commitment to sincerely follow Christ. Because I didn't truly know Him, I couldn't truly revere Him. I didn't think it was a big deal to use His name in that way. It was normal for me, and common for society to misuse His name as well. Many times I didn't even realize what I was saying. Yet, as I drew closer to Him and began to fall in love with His character, my respect for Him blossomed. As my respect blossomed, His name became so precious to me that I only wanted to speak it in a worthy manner.

This is the difference between true heart change and behavior modification. Heart change is God's goal with each and every one of us. Not rules and rituals. Not a list of do's and don'ts. Not to coerce us with guilt and punishment. Instead, His goal is that our souls would be so connected to His and our relationship so strong, we would desire to please and obey Him above all else. He longs for us to cherish His name, His Word, His church, and His commands. As we pursue Him, reverent behavior will come naturally because our hearts will belong to Him. Our love will empower our obedience and God will make His home in our spirits.

"Whoever has my commandments and keeps them, he it is who loves me. And he who loves me will be loved by my Father, and I will love him and manifest myself to him." John 14:21 ESV

Personal Reflection:

Do my words and actions reflect the faith I profess? Is my respect for God revealed in my conduct?

Is my heart fully surrendered to God? Am I willing to give Him first place with my time and my priorities?

Does the way I approach church and the way I use God's name show reverence for Him? Why or why not?

Heavenly Father, we come to You as women who deeply desire to know You and to live out Your will. We pray You will reveal to us any area of our lives where our words or actions do not reflect our faith. We want to be women who respect and honor You in all things. We know to be this kind of woman, You need to have first place in our hearts. Help us to put You where you belong in our lives. To prioritize our relationship with You above all else. To give You our best, always. Empower us by Your precious grace to be obedient to You and to live up to everything You have created us to be. Let the way we approach Your church speak of our reverence for You. Let the way we use Your name reflect our deep admiration for who You are. Forgive us for the times we have misused Your name or disrespected Your church. May all that we say and do point to You. May our reverence for You be seen by all. In Jesus precious name, Amen.

Chapter 3
Created to Speak Life

Older women likewise are to be...not slanderers.
Titus 2:3 ESV

Slander: "The action or crime of making a false spoken
statement damaging to a person's reputation."

God created us to be women whose words will uplift
and encourage those who hear them. We are called to
build others up and to talk about people in a way that
honors God and reflects His love. The Greek word Paul used
here in this passage gives remarkable depth to what it truly
means to be a slanderer. The word used was *diabolos*, which
translates in Strong's Concordance: "The devil, to accuse, a
false accuser. In the New Testament, the ho diabolos appears
as the constant enemy of God, of Christ, of the divine
kingdom, or the followers of Christ and of all truth; full of
falsehood and malice, and seducing to evil in every possible
way."

I was stunned when I discovered that the Lord equates
slandering to being of the devil! I believe we have a tendency
to view gossip/slander as some sort of "lesser sin", yet it is
clear God does not view it this way. A slanderer is said
biblically to be malicious, evil, and an enemy of God.

If we want to live a life that brings honor to our Creator, we
must choose our words wisely when we speak about others.
When we speak falsely, or when we speak negative words that

can damage a person's reputation, we do not reflect the glory of God as we were designed to do. Even if our words are true in our own perspective; our opinion is not always reality. We view people and circumstances through our own filters, processed through the lenses of our emotions, which is why two people describing the same situation will often have very different stories.

Do not speak evil against one another, brothers. The one who speaks against a brother or judges his brother, speaks evil against the law and judges the law. James 4:11 ESV

Slandering and gossiping are very closely related. In fact, the word gossiper is described biblically as a whisperer, or secret slanderer. I know gossiping can be a struggle for many women. It's something in my own life I've had to fight against. The way we speak about others reveals our hearts. When our hearts are full of love and the grace of God, we will believe the best about people. We will seek to amplify their strengths and positive qualities while overlooking their weaknesses. We will use our words to build up, rather than tear down.

"The good person out of the good treasure of his heart produces good, and the evil person out of his evil treasure produces evil, for out of the abundance of the heart his mouth speaks." Luke 6:45 ESV

Jesus spoke of this concept often, especially to the Pharisees (religious leaders of the day). The Pharisees were so careful to abide by every minute detail of the Jewish law, yet their hearts remained unchanged. This was revealed in how they treated and spoke about others. They condemned Jesus and His disciples as being defiled because they didn't follow scrupulous washing rituals before eating.

This gave Jesus the perfect opportunity to teach them a lesson about what truly defiled a person.

And he said, "What comes out of a person is what defiles him. For from within, out of the heart of man, come evil thoughts, sexual immorality, theft, murder, adultery, coveting, wickedness, deceit, sensuality, envy, slander, pride, foolishness. All these evil things come from within, and they defile a person." Mark 7:20-23 ESV

When we are intentional about filling our hearts with God's love, grace, and mercy, those same attributes will overflow into our conversations. Our lips will speak what our hearts are full of. We will begin to notice that the less we gossip or speak negatively about people, the more peace we will have. Gossiping not only paints others in a bad light, it is physically and mentally draining to us as well. Our words create a toxic atmosphere that can suck the life right out of us. On the flip side, positivity breeds positivity. A woman who follows Christ has the power to speak God's love and light into every conversation. We have the ability and the responsibility to be life-givers with our words.

Do not let any unwholesome talk come out of your mouths, but only what is helpful for building others up according to their needs, that it may benefit those who listen.
Ephesians 4:29 ESV

The Bible contrasts two people who make drastically different choices with their words. The wise person is trustworthy and keeps secrets. This person restrains his or her lips from speaking about others. They are described as being a seeker of love, for love covers over a multitude of sins. The foolish person, on the other hand, goes about slandering others. This person is a secret whisperer, and in so doing, she tears apart friendships and spread conflict. We have a choice every day and every conversation to decide which person we will be.

If gossiping is a struggle for you, this may be difficult at first. Yet, as you proactively seek Jesus it will begin to come naturally. Every time an intentional decision is made that you will be the wise person discussed above, gossip will loosen its hold. Remind yourself daily that death and life are in the power of the tongue. As James says, our tongues are small but powerful. And difficult to be tamed!

For every kind of beast and bird, of reptile and sea creature, can be tamed and has been tamed by mankind, but no human being can tame the tongue. It is a restless evil, full of deadly poison. With it we bless our Lord and Father, and with it we curse people who are made in the likeness of God. From the same mouth come blessing and cursing. My brothers, these things ought not to be so. James 3:7-10 ESV

The difference I've noticed in my life from applying these truths has been profound. I no longer feed into the enemy's attempts to get me involved in other people's business. Without gossip to fuel the fire, conflict dies down quickly. Because of this, I have experienced abundant peace. I pray you will experience the fruits of obedience to these Scriptures in your own life. Keep in mind, God is always listening. Every word we speak. Every conversation (whether to one person or to a hundred). Every text. Every social media post. Nothing is hidden from Him.

We were designed to be women whose words would reflect God's loving Spirit that lives inside of us. The Message version of the Bible says it like this, "Words kill, words give life; they're either poison or fruit – you choose." Let's choose wisely! Before we speak let's ask ourselves these questions: Is what I am about to say true, necessary, and kind? Will this statement honor Christ? What is my motive for saying this? If these questions cannot be answered in a positive way, the smart choice would be to keep silent. We should daily ask for God's help to keep our words pure.

Set a guard over my mouth Lord; keep watch over the door of my lips. Psalm 141:3 ESV

We were created to be women whose faith is evident in the words we speak. May our words be loving, grace-filled, life-giving, and healing. With God's help, our tongues can be used for good and not evil. Let the words we speak reflect His goodness at all times, and in so doing, draw others to His marvelous love.

Personal Reflection:
Do my words bring grace to those who hear them? Do I use them to speak life, positivity, and encouragement to others?

What kind of conversations am I typically involved in? Do I discuss other people's affairs? How can I be intentional about redirecting my conversations towards those most honoring to God?

Can I say at all times that my words are reflecting the love of Christ? If the answer is no, what changes need to be made?

Heavenly Father, as women who seek to honor You, let our words be pure, noble, good, and always pleasing to You. Help us to truly believe the best about people, and amplify their strengths while downplaying their weaknesses. Help us to always consider the impact our words will have on the lives of others. Forgive us when we have gossiped, slandered, or in any way spoken negatively about another person. Convict us when our conversations begin to drift in a manner that will be dishonoring to You. Help us to be conscious of every word we speak, not speaking carelessly, but instead careful to honor You in everything we say. Empower us to be life givers who will breathe positivity and goodness into every conversation. May we always use our words to uplift and build one another up. May we speak with tongues of grace, bringing honor and glory to Your name. In the words of the Psalmist David, "May the words of our lips and the meditations of our hearts be pleasing to You, Oh Lord, our Rock and our Redeemer." In Jesus precious name, Amen.

Chapter 4
Created to be Filled with God's Spirit

Women are not to be ... slaves to much wine.
Titus 2:3 ESV

Every single woman on this planet was created to live in close relationship with her Heavenly Father. Sadly, many of us turn to substances to fill the empty space inside that only God can fill. We forsake Jesus, the fountain of living water that replenishes us from the inside, and instead attempt to quench our spiritual thirst externally. This leaves us empty and always craving more.

Wine is a good gift from the Father to be enjoyed in moderation, yet this gift has been twisted and misused by the enemy in countless ways. Many look to alcohol to satisfy them in a way that only God truly can, leading to destruction and chaos. Alcohol abuse is out of control in our society. Here are some sobering statistics in 2018 from the NIAAA:

· Each year, 30% of driving fatalities will be due to an alcohol impaired driver.
· 15 million people in the United States struggle with alcohol abuse
· Teen alcohol use kills 4,700 people per year.
· 80,000 deaths per year are attributed to alcohol use.

Wine is a mocker, strong drink a brawler, and whoever is led astray by it is not wise. Proverbs 20:1 ESV

I have firsthand witnessed the damage and destruction alcohol can cause. Drug and alcohol abuse runs rampant in my family. I have seen alcohol destroy homes, damage relationships, and take the lives of loved ones. Growing up with parents who abused drugs and alcohol has left lifelong scars on my heart. I still deal with the effects of it today. In His mercy, the Lord rescued me out of repeating the same mistakes as my parents. He took me off of a path that surely would have led to addiction and destruction, and for that I am so grateful.

Many think that God is out to steal all of our fun, and Christianity is just a long list of do's and don'ts. This could not be further from the truth, for Jesus said:

"The thief comes only to steal and kill and destroy. I came so that they may have life and have it abundantly."
John 10:10 ESV

Jesus came so we could have abundant life! He isn't trying to take our happiness. He wants to instill in us the everlasting joy only *He* can bring. Happiness is circumstantial, joy is constant and eternal. Knowing and obeying Jesus as Lord brings a deep joy that does not waver with the ups and downs of life and the changing of circumstances. The rules God puts into place are not meant to be uncomfortably restricting, they are boundaries meant to keep us safe.

Our Heavenly Father knows the devastation alcohol abuse can cause. Pain and heartache. Immorality and regret. Sickness and death. As our Creator, He knows what is good for our souls and what is not. Life works best when we follow His guidelines. Over and over, Scripture warns us about drunkenness.

Woe to those who rise early in the morning, that they may run after strong drink, who tarry late into the evening as wine inflames them! Isaiah 5:11 ESV

And do not get drunk with wine, for that is debauchery, but be filled with the Spirit, addressing one another in psalms and hymns and spiritual songs, singing and making melody to the Lord with your heart. Ephesians 5:18-19 ESV

For you have spent enough time in the past doing what pagans choose to do –living in debauchery, lust, drunkenness, orgies, carousing, and detestable idolatry. 1 Peter 3:3 NIV

We were created to be women who would recognize God's reign over every area of our lives. Women who would set our minds to obey because we acknowledge that God knows best. As we seek God with all of our hearts, we will become this type of woman. Our desire will be to live a life that is pleasing to our Creator. We will aspire to honor God every minute, every hour, every day. This will extend past being merely "Sunday morning Christians". Our faith will become evident daily, in every choice we make. Turning down drinks may make us seem a little odd in a culture that is saturated with alcohol but remember, we were created to be different! If people think we are strange, we are probably doing something right.

Unless God has given you specific conviction to completely abstain from alcohol, biblically it is perfectly ok to enjoy a drink safely and in moderation. Don't forget to give thanks to the Lord for this as well! God loves a heart that is grateful for all of His gifts.

Go eat your bread with joy, and drink your wine with a merry heart. Ecclesiastes 9:7a ESV

You cause the grass to grow for the livestock and plants for man to cultivate, that he may bring forth food from the earth and wine to gladden the heart of man.. Psalm 104:14-15 ESV

If the Lord has allowed you to exercise your freedom in this area, always be conscious of how your actions will affect another. If your choice to have a glass of wine in front of someone who has felt conviction not to drink will cause them to stumble, the other person should always be put first. It is better to abstain than to offend another believer.

But take care that this right of yours does not somehow become a stumbling block to the weak. 1 Corinthians 8:9 ESV

For those with whom alcohol addiction runs in the family, or who have had issues with alcohol in the past, it is usually best to give up alcohol completely. Why give the devil a foothold into your life? If alcohol abuse is something you struggle with, know that you are not alone! I spent much of my life looking to fill the God–shaped void in my heart with alcohol. I looked for happiness in all the wrong places, through partying and wild living. This created a brief satisfaction that would never last. Synthetic happiness that eventually came crashing down around me as the buzz wore off. Only after being rescued off of that path by Jesus, can I truly see it for the empty and soul-sucking lifestyle that it was.

I now possess a true joy that never goes away. I have a peace that is impossible to find in a pill or at the bottom of a bottle. Being drunk does not compare in the slightest bit to being close to the Lord Jesus and filled with His Spirit, I promise you that. To those who think life could not possibly be exciting without alcohol, I can testify that my life is anything but boring! True Christianity is the most amazing adventure as we partner with God and help Him advance His kingdom on earth.

My days are filled with excitement and awe as I grow closer to my Creator and see Him work wonders in my life and the lives of those I love.

When Jesus rescues someone from a lifestyle such as mine, a deep love and appreciation for Him will always be the result. I shudder to think what my story would have been like had He not intervened. I certainly wouldn't be here today, writing this book and using my gifts for God's glory. I am so grateful He stepped in before I ruined my own life, and in so doing, the lives of my loved ones. What the devil tried to destroy in me, God has redeemed and restored! He took a small mustard seed of faith and grew it into something amazing. He has rewarded my commitment to seeking Him and putting Him first with a completely transformed life.

He had a plan for me all along, just as He has a plan for you, Friend! The Bible tells the story of a sinful woman who was so grateful to be in the presence of Jesus that she wept profusely. As she did, she knelt to kiss His feet and wipe the tears off with her hair. As His companions looked on, appalled, Jesus silenced them with His words, affirming the woman's actions.

Then He turned toward the woman and said to Simon, "Do you see this woman? I came into your house. You did not give me any water for my feet, but she wet my feet with her tears and wiped them with her hair. You did not give me a kiss, but this woman, from the time I entered, has not stopped kissing my feet. You did not put oil on my head, but she has poured perfume on my feet. Therefore, I tell you, her many sins have been forgiven – as her great love has shown. But whoever has been forgiven little loves little." Luke 7:44-47 NIV

The amazing forgiveness of Jesus is available to every single one of us, no matter how far we have fallen or how much of a mess we have made with our lives. Through Him, those who have struggled with substance abuse will be given strength to overcome. As we surrender and draw close to Him, His victory becomes ours. He transforms us from the inside out.

He has completely changed all of my desires. He replaced all of my passion for partying with a passion for pursuing Him instead.

If this is your struggle as well, receive His forgiveness today. Lay all of your burdens at His feet, and He will give you the strength to overcome. You will experience victory and freedom beyond your wildest imagination!

Now the Lord is the Spirit, and where the Spirit of the Lord is there is freedom. 2 Corinthians 3:17 ESV

Personal Reflection:

Do I use alcohol safely and in moderation? Does my behavior consistently honor God whether I am having a drink or not?

Do I look to alcohol to fill me in a way that only Jesus can? Am I willing to set this habit aside and seek fulfillment from God and God alone?

Do I sense the Lord's conviction to abstain from alcohol due to family history, personal history, or for reasons unknown?

Heavenly Father, our deep and heartfelt desire is to please You in all things. Let us be women who honor You in every area of our lives. We know the boundaries You set in place are there for our protection. We know life works best when we follow Your rules. We acknowledge You as Lord over all. Help us to stand strong in the face of opposition and temptation. Help us in any areas of weakness. Remove ungodly influences from our lives and surround us with women who also revere and honor Your Word. We pray for those who are struggling with substance abuse. We ask that You would fill them to the fullest with Your love and joy. May they turn to You for comfort, peace, and satisfaction, rather than to alcohol or drugs. We pray that Your forgiveness would be received by every person reading this prayer. We pray for family members caught in the cycle of addiction. Lord that You would break strongholds and set them free. We ask that You would turn their lives completely around for their good and Your glory. In Jesus precious name, Amen.

Chapter 5

Created to be an Example

*They are to teach what is good, and so train the young
women. Titus 2:3 ESV*

Each one of us has been created to live a life of
significance and influence, one that sets an example for
others to follow. Our lives hold the power to paint a
beautiful picture of what living in close relationship with Jesus
looks like. This Scripture specifically directs older women to
guide the younger. While we would typically think the word
young is only referencing age, the original Greek word shows
differently.

The Greek word used here for young was *neos*, which does
mean youthful; but it also implies being "young in the faith,
fresh; renewed in heart, nature, and disposition." By this
definition we see that God is instructing us, as believing
women, to seek out those who are newer believers, young in
the faith, and teach them how to live a life pleasing to Him.

*Show yourself in all respects to be a model of good works, and
in your teaching show integrity, dignity, and sound speech.
Titus 2:7-8a ESV*

While some women are given the specific spiritual gift of
teaching, we are all called to model what it looks like to follow
Jesus. By example we do this as we live out our faith
obediently for all to see. Yet we should also be intentional to

seek out specific women that need our help. This involves commitment on our part, and fully investing in and sharing our lives with other women. Doing life together. Celebrating victories and praying together through the hard times.

Something important God has taught me along this journey is I have to let go of my perfectionism in order to help those who are new in the faith. I am definitely far from perfect. I struggle to obey at times. I wrestle with my faith and I have valley moments where I strain to see the goodness of God.

Do I have good days, when God is so near and I'm walking in obedience to Him while literally feeling His presence all around me? Absolutely! But do I also have days where I choose to sin by complaining or losing my temper, thus grieving the Holy Spirit and provoking the Lord's discipline? Yes! If I only share my victories and my mountain-top moments, that's just not real life. Other women won't be able to relate to me because they aren't perfect either. We are just imperfect people helping each other to look more and more like the only perfect one: Jesus.

The Rock, His work is perfect, for all His ways are justice. A God of faithfulness and without iniquity, just and upright is He. Deuteronomy 32:4 ESV

Jesus is the only perfect one. It's His obedience that brings us peace with God and our Christianity will be a lifelong process of growing to look more and more like Him. As we grow, and we help others, we must remember to be gracious. To ourselves and to those we influence. The goal is progress, not perfection. As we actively pursue Jesus we will be changed, from one degree of glory to another. This does not happen instantly, it is a process. We want all the spiritual maturity in ourselves and others right now! (At least I know I do.) But God doesn't work that way. Sanctification is on His schedule, in His timing.

Yes we cooperate, but it's His work in our hearts that produces the growth. Trust the process.

For it is God who works in you, both to will and to work for His good pleasure. Philippians 2:13 ESV

To live out the command of training other women, t
he first and most crucial step is to make certain we are daily filling ourselves up with Jesus. Spending time worshipping, praying, and reading our Bibles. We can't give out what we don't possess. To teach the Spirit-filled life, we need to be filled with the Spirit. To disciple other women in following Jesus, we must first be disciples ourselves.

"Go therefore and make disciples of all nations, baptizing them in the name of the Father and of the Son and of the Holy Spirit, teaching them to observe all that I have commanded you"... Matthew 28:20 ESV

Time with God needs to be our top priority. May we never forget there is an enemy of our souls who would like nothing more than to distract us and keep us too busy to seek God. This enemy loves to keep us focused on temporary pleasures rather than pursuing eternal rewards. Even seemingly good activities can be detrimental if they occupy time that should belong to the Lord. We should be wary of anything that takes God's rightful place in our lives. Seek Him first and all else will follow.

O Lord, in the morning you hear my voice; in the morning I prepare a sacrifice for you and watch. Psalm 5:3 ESV

Satisfy us in the morning with your steadfast love, that we may rejoice and be glad all our days. Psalm 90:14 ESV

Giving God the first portion of our day not only shows Him we are serious about putting Him first, it allows us to be filled with His Spirit before we encounter anyone else. This is so important if we want to live and teach a lifestyle that honors God. In my own experience, the days I have been too rushed and have skipped my morning devotion time have resulted in a more irritable and less peaceful demeanor. On those days I am more reactive and less contemplative before I speak. Through years of discipline, and some not so easily learned lessons, I have begun to orient my days around my morning time. I try to allow myself plenty of time between when I wake for the day and when I schedule my first activity, and lately it's been before anyone else in the house wakes up. I've found this to be the absolute best time to be still and focus on listening to the Lord. As seasons change and schedules change, I adjust to make sure God gets first priority.

When we make a conscious effort to put God first, He will show us how to make time for Him. This may mean waking up earlier to dedicate to Him the first portion of our day. It may mean staying up late to finish a Bible study. It may involve spending less time on social media so that we can do devotions instead.

On super hectic days when the unexpected occurs, the kids don't cooperate, or well, life happens, we can stay connected in other ways. My favorite way to stay in tune with God is to listen to praise and worship music throughout the day. This keeps my heart focused on God and allows me to express my gratitude to Him and give Him praise. I also will listen to sermons or watch short video teachings when I have spare time, or while I'm working around the house. It is vital that we stay close to God through constant prayer and communication. Time spent with Him needs to be as essential to our lives as food and water. It must be this way for every believer. Jesus referred to Himself as the living water when He said:

"Everyone who drinks of this water will be thirsty again, but whoever drinks of the water that I will give him will never be thirsty again. The water that I will give him will become in him a spring of water welling up to eternal life."
John 4:13-14 ESV

To illustrate the importance of prioritizing time with God, let's look at the story of Martha and Mary. These two sisters welcomed Jesus into their home and Martha immediately got busy making preparations for serving dinner. Mary, instead, sat at Jesus' feet and soaked up His precious teachings. After some time, a very frazzled and agitated Martha complained to Jesus that her sister was leaving all the burden of work on her. To which Jesus stressed to her the importance of putting Him above all else. When we, like Mary, seek God first, everything else will flow from that. We will then be able to go about our days with the peace in our souls which only comes from spending time with Him.

But the Lord answered her, "Martha, Martha, you are anxious and troubled about many things, but one thing is necessary. Mary has chosen the good portion, which will not be taken away from her." Luke 10:41-42 ESV

Apart from Jesus we can do nothing. We come to Him to be replenished. We come to Him when we are tired and weary. We come to Him for His Word and His Presence, for in them we find fullness of life. He guides our lives and makes straight our paths. We must come to Him and drink deeply of His living water so that it can overflow to everyone around us. We can't pour from an empty cup. He fills us and we fill others. Everything we go through, every trial and every struggle, has the potential to encourage somebody else. I can't even count how many times God has used the difficulties I have gone through to encourage and comfort someone else.

Paul spoke of this same experience when he wrote to the believers in Corinth:

Blessed be the God and Father of our Lord Jesus Christ, the Father of mercies and God of all comfort, who comforts us in our affliction, so that we may be able to comfort those who are in any affliction, with the comfort with which we ourselves are comforted by God. 2 Corinthians 1:3-4 ESV

God's intention for us as believers is to pour into each other's lives. To comfort and to encourage. To teach and to train. To build each other up as we journey along God's path, looking forward to the day when Jesus returns and all is made right with the world. Be intentional about each day and seek God's will for you in that day. He will give you direction and the very specific guidance that you need when you seek Him daily.

Ask Him specifically to bring other women into your life that are new in the faith, or seeking to know more about Christ. He will answer those prayers. When He does, be that woman who embodies grace and truth as you lead others. Focus your efforts on becoming a godly woman and then teach everything you are learning to someone else. Be a shining light for Jesus and make every day count for the Kingdom.

Personal Reflection:

Am I filling myself with God daily so that I can pour into the life of another? If the answer is no, what is taking God's place and what changes can I make?

Do I give grace to others and allow them room to make mistakes and to grow? Do I offer this same grace to myself?

Who has God placed in my life that I can actively seek to mentor?

Heavenly Father, we thank You for Your precious Word and for the opportunity to represent You on this earth. We are so grateful You work in our hearts to produce right living and we want to cooperate with You in every way that we can. Help us to orient our schedules and our lives so that You get top priority. Show us areas where we are devoting our time to lesser pursuits. Help us to identify anything that is taking Your place, consuming time that should belong to You. Give us Your living water, our daily bread that is crucial and necessary for each day. Help us to remember the story of Martha and Mary, and remind ourselves to always choose You, our good portion. Fill us up with Your goodness so we can fill others. Bring women our way who we can influence and train in Your ways. Help us to embody Jesus' teachings and draw others to His marvelous love. Surround us with those who need Your love the most. May we be models of Your grace and truth. May we leave every woman we encounter with a glimpse of Your heart. In Jesus mighty name, Amen.

Chapter 6
Created to Love

Train the young women...to love their husbands and children.
Titus 2:4 ESV

We are called to love our husbands and children. This may seem like an obvious point, but let's dig a little deeper into what the Bible says about love. (If you aren't yet a wife or mama, keep reading there's something here for you too!) There are two Greek words most commonly used to define love in the New Testament. These words are *phileo* and *agape*. Two different kinds of love, both laid out for believers to emulate. Although this particular passage refers to *phileo* love, we will discuss both types of love and how we can express them; because both are vital in the life of a believer.

Here is a brief description of *phileo* love according to Strong's Concordance: "A friendly love, to be fond of, to have affection for. Love expressed in affection and warmth towards another." *Phileo* love is best described as affectionate and generous love that seeks to make the other person happy. This type of love focuses more on feelings, and how we communicate those feelings to one another. Think of *phileo* love as warm and fuzzy love, expressing itself in how we treat the other person. This is the way we are to love our husbands and children. They should feel as if they are our prized possessions and the object of our affections. We should lavish love on them continually and without restraint.

We can express this love by seeking out ways to make them happy, being affectionate physically, and using words that clearly portray our love for them. We should tell our husbands and children we love them often. It's amazing what a kind word or a gentle touch can do for a person. This may be difficult for someone who wasn't used to this kind of affectionate love growing up, and for those who don't respond well to this kind of love. If loving in this way is a struggle for you, I recommend spending some time in prayer and seeking the Lord's wisdom for the reason why, and His wisdom on how to overcome. He will help you to heal on the inside so that you can express this type of love externally.

A key component in making sure our husband and children feel loved is to learn about the love languages. There are five common love languages, which are ways we give and receive love. Everyone is different. Some respond best to words of affirmation; they need to be built up and affirmed verbally to feel loved. Others respond best to gifts; receiving gifts makes them feel thought about and loved. Another love language is acts of service. This person feels loved when their partner does things for them. The last two are quality time (time spent = love) and physical touch (affection = love).

When we discover the love language of our husbands and children, we can commit to expressing their unique kind of love to them. We should also know our own love language. Usually the way we express love is the love language that we require. My love language is words of affirmation. It makes me feel loved when my husband builds me up with his words. This is also one of the primary ways I express my love. We, as wives, can be under the impression that we are expressing love because we are giving love the way we receive it. But if it isn't our husbands' specific love language, there will be a disconnect. Same goes for children. It's important we find out how each person in our family best receives love, so we can always make sure they are feeling loved by us.

The second type of love used in the Bible was *agape* love. This was the most commonly used form of love in Scripture, and the kind that is requested of all believers towards all people.

"A new commandment I give to you, that you love one another: just as I have loved you, you also are to love one another. By this all people will know that you are my disciples, if you have love for one another."
John 13: 34-35 ESV

This love that Jesus requires of His followers is only possible by the power of the Holy Spirit. While *phileo* love can be portrayed by believers and unbelievers alike, *agape* love can only come from its source: God. *Agape* love is the nature and expression of God's character. God is love, and therefore He loves. It is unconditional and undeserving love. It is the kind of love that prompted the Father to sacrifice His very Son for us. This love manifests in intentional goodwill, benevolence, and delight towards another. Faithful and committed. Sacrificial. Loving in this manner requires the supernatural strength of the Holy Spirit.

But the fruit of the Spirit is love. Galatians 5:22a ESV

Agape love is a fruit of the Spirit. We cannot produce this type of love on our own. This kind of sacrificial love is a byproduct of a heart and a life completely surrendered to God. As we seek Him and grow, this love will manifest in our lives. We cannot muster up the strength to love this way on our own. By nature, it is impossible to love others the way God loves us. But with God, all things are possible. As He works in our lives, we will see this and many other fruits of the Spirit (characteristics of Christ manifested by God's work in our hearts) grow in our lives.

I have experienced this supernatural kind of love in my own life. As I've grown closer to God, my love for others has also grown. My natural tendency to be self-centered and self-serving has turned into a passion for loving others and putting them first.

True love for God will always express itself in sacrificial love for others. This is evidence of His Spirit working in and through us.

Beloved, let us love one another, for love is from God and whoever loves has been born of God and knows God. Anyone who does not love does not know God, because God is love. In this the love of God was made manifest among us, that God sent His only Son into the world, so that we might live through him. Beloved, if God so loved us, we also ought to love one another. No one has ever seen God; if we love one another, God abides in us and his love is perfected in us. 1 John 4:7-9,11 ESV

John was not referring to worldly love when He wrote this letter. He was not referring to our concept of love, a fickle love that wavers with the circumstances. Nor was he referring to the *phileo* love that we are specifically asked to bestow upon our husbands and children. Instead, he spoke of the *agape* love which only comes from the Father, and which exists in the hearts of all believers. This is how others will know we belong to Jesus. We love because He loved us first. Our love moves us to compassionate action and selfless giving. This starts in our homes, with our husbands and children, and extends to everyone, everywhere. No one is exempt from receiving this type of love from us, not even our enemies.

"But I say to you, Love your enemies and pray for those who persecute you, so that you may be sons of your Father, who is in Heaven." Matthew 5:44-45 ESV

I don't know about you, but personally; loving my enemies requires a supernatural strength only God can give. To be completely honest, sometimes loving my family also requires this strength. (Can I get a witness?) Loving unconditionally and sacrificially is difficult. But thankfully, the Lord never asks us to do something He doesn't equip us to do. Staying close to His side and abiding in His love empowers and enables us to pass this love on to others. As God's daughters, let's meditate upon these love Scriptures and ask our Father to give us the power and strength to live them out. He will be faithful to help us shine with the love of Jesus as we were beautifully designed to do!

Love is patient and kind; love does not envy or boast; it is not arrogant or rude. It does not insist on its own way; it is not irritable or resentful; it does not rejoice at wrongdoing, but rejoices with the truth. Love bears all things, believes all things, endures all things. 1 Corinthians 13:4-7

Personal Reflection:
Would I be able to replace the word love in the above Scriptures with my name? If I say this out loud does it ring true? (Ex: Amy is patient, Amy is kind). How can I adjust my attitude and actions to be obedient to these words?

Am I showing my husband/children *phileo* and *agape* love? What is one thing I can do today to display my love for them?

What are the love languages of my family members? How can I express my love in the best way for them to receive it?

Heavenly Father, we come to You humbly knowing it is impossible to love the way You want us to love without Your help. We know sometimes our tendencies are the complete opposite of loving. We ask that You give us hearts to love like Jesus. Infuse us with Your love. Pour love into our hearts so that we can display it to others. Strengthen us with Your Word and Your truth. May our loving lives be a testimony to Your grace and goodness. Forgive us for the times we have been unloving to our husbands and children. Although they deserve the best of us, they often get the worst. Make us quick to apologize when we act in unloving ways. Give us wisdom to love them the way they need to be loved. Help us to identify their love languages so we can love them in the best way possible. Give us the strength and patience to love everyone You have placed in our lives, including our enemies. May Your kindness always abound in our hearts. In Jesus precious name we pray. Amen.

Chapter 7
Created to Withstand Temptation

Train the young women...to be self controlled.
Titus 2:5 ESV

God calls us to be women of great composure and self control. A self-controlled woman is said biblically to be moderate in opinion and not to be ruled by any sinful desires. She is composed, self-disciplined, and has a steadiness and sobriety about her that is noticeable. This woman is not excessive in any area of her life. She is not one to be led by her carnal nature.

This means she is not controlled by her own wants and desires which, at times, can be in contrast to God's will. Rather, she is a woman who is led by the Spirit. Her main desire is to be close to Jesus, and live so that His name will be glorified in her life. She stands against temptation and does not give in. This is the type of woman we should aspire to become as we grow as Christ-followers. We have the power to live this way because of the power that lives in us.

For God gave us a spirit not of fear but of power and love and self-control. 2 Timothy 1:7 ESV

In order to have a more complete understanding of our spirit nature vs. our carnal (or fleshly) nature, let's look at the book of Romans. Those who have not turned to Christ are said to be led by their flesh. The Greek word for flesh, *sarx*, explains this nature as having a "proneness to sin; it is a carnal nature driven by sinful passions and affections." The person led by their flesh is focused on gratifying their desires constantly. They only think about the here and now. They do not possess an eternity-based mindset. They have no control over their sinful nature; instead, they are controlled by *it* in every way. This was every single one of us before we repented and placed faith in Christ; thereby receiving forgiveness of sin, peace with God, and a new Spirit which dwells in us. This Spirit, God's Holy Spirit, equips and enables us to live righteously and put sin to death in our lives. It is by His Spirit that we are set free from sin and empowered to live for God.

But thanks be to God, that you who were once slaves of sin have become obedient from the heart to the standard of teaching to which you were committed, and having been set free from sin, have become slaves of righteousness.
Romans 7:17-18 ESV

So, because of this new nature we are instantly free from every sin and will never struggle with sinful passions because we are holy and led by the Spirit. Kidding!! I wish this were true but unfortunately the Christian life is a struggle. A struggle between our new Spirit-filled nature, and our old fleshly nature. Think of these two natures at constant war with each other. While we are not controlled by sinful desires and led by our flesh once we put our faith in Christ, that doesn't mean this nature won't pop up constantly. Paul explains this in more detail to the Romans.

So I find it to be a law that when I want to do right, evil lies close at hand. For I delight in the law of God, in my inner being, but I see in my members another law waging war against the law of my mind and making me captive to the law of sin that dwells in my members. Wretched man that I am!

Who will deliver me from this body of death? Thanks be to
God through Jesus Christ our Lord! Romans 7:21-25 ESV

Praise Jesus as our great Deliverer! Through Him we have
the power to overcome every sin, break every chain, and tear
down every stronghold. There is victory in His name! The
very same power that raised Christ from the dead now lives in
us and, because of this; we are no longer slaves to our desires.
This is the Spirit-filled life we are infused with. A life of peace,
love, joy, and self-control.

But if Christ is in you, although the body is dead because of
sin, the Spirit is life because of righteousness. If the Spirit of
Him who raised Jesus from the dead dwells in you, He who
raised Christ Jesus from the dead will also give life to your
mortal bodies through His Spirit who dwells in you.
Romans 8:10-11 ESV

This all sounds fantastic when we read it in Scripture but,
practically speaking, how do we live a life that is led by the
Spirit? How do we win the battle between our two natures
and become the women God created us to be? We set our
minds on the things of the Spirit rather than the things of the
flesh. This involves feeding our spirits by choosing to spend
our free time praying, reading our Bibles, and getting to know
Jesus. We abide in Him and He gives us the strength to be the
women we were designed to be.

We, in biblical terms, crucify our flesh by refusing to
indulge in what it wants. Whether our particular indulgence is
in food, shopping, lustful behaviors; the less we give in to
these passions, the weaker their strongholds become. As we
continually surrender every area to Christ, His Spirit will
begin to work in our lives, to our benefit and His glory. The
more time we spend with Him, the more led by the Spirit we
will be.

But I say, walk by the Spirit, and you will not gratify the desires of the flesh. Galatians 5:16 ESV

There are also practical steps we must take as we partner with God to overcome sin. God does not do all the work; it is a joint effort between us and the Spirit. We need to identify areas of temptation and weakness and put a plan into place to help eradicate them. It is not enough to just hope we will be strong enough to resist temptation if we keep putting ourselves in the same situations that trigger our sinful passions.

But each person is tempted when they are dragged away by their own evil desires and enticed. James 1:14 ESV

In my own life an area I struggled to gain control over early on in my walk with the Lord was my drinking and ungodly language and behavior. I would pray for God to enable me to withstand the temptation to go along with the crowd, yet all the while I would continue to place myself in the same situations with the same people. It was only after those friendships were removed from my life that I realized the only way to be sure I would resist temptation would be to stop putting myself in tempting situations. I had to avoid certain people and certain circumstances until God made me strong enough to be the light and remain steadfast in my loyalty to Him. Now, the desire to act that way is completely gone, and those temptations no longer hold any allure for me.

If our struggles are similar, a practical step for you would be to distance yourself from friends who are not walking with God, and refuse invitations that you know would be dishonoring to Him. Seek out godly friendships that will sharpen you and encourage you to live for Jesus. Pray for God to bring these friendships into your life. He will be faithful to answer that prayer. If your temptation is shopping, a practical step for you might be to cut up credit cards and remove shopping apps from your phone. If you lose your self control and tend to be super opinionated and extreme on social media, it may be time to log off for a while and seek the Lord in your free time instead.

When our particular temptation surfaces, we must remember to counteract it with the word of God! Know that the enemy waits and watches for just the right time to strike. If we are ill-prepared for his attacks, we will be easy prey. Staying close to the Lord by prioritizing time with Him will keep us on guard. Having a thorough knowledge of His Word will keep us prepared for whatever the enemy throws our way. There is no better example of this than Jesus' own temptation in the wilderness.

After fasting for forty days and nights Jesus was understandably hungry. The enemy watched and waited. He knew when Jesus was at His weakest point, hungry and weary. The enemy watched, he waited, and then he pounced. He slyly suggested for Jesus to turn stones into bread to satisfy His hunger. He invited Jesus to throw Himself down from the temple to prove that He was the Son of God.

Each temptation was intended to lure Jesus off the path God had marked out for Him. Rather than succumb to the devil's lies, Jesus spoke the word of God to him multiple times and the enemy left. I think it's interesting to note that immediately after this point Jesus began His ministry and chose His disciples. Our greatest blessings often come after we have resisted our greatest temptations.

Therefore put on the full armor of God , so that when the day of evil comes, you may be able to stand your ground, and after you have done everything, to stand. Ephesians 6:13 ESV

If there is an area in your life where you are prone to excess, or a vice you feel you have no control over, remember that in

Jesus you have the power to overcome. The Bible is full of Scriptures that speak to this part of your identity. Don't live a defeated life, a slave to your temptations and denying the power that lives inside of you. Rise up and declare victory over your situation, in Jesus name!

Personal Reflection:
Would I consider myself a self-controlled woman? Am I composed and even-tempered? In assessing my life and habits, do I appear to be led by the Spirit or led by the flesh? Why or why not?

Do I exercise restraint in all areas of my life?

What are my particular temptations? What practical steps can I take to remove temptation from my life? Which Scriptures would be helpful to memorize when fighting off these temptations?

Heavenly Father, thank You so much for Your constant guidance. We are so grateful You lead us with Your loving hand into all truth and righteousness. Please shine Your light of truth into our hearts and lives to expose the areas that need to align with Your Word. Bring to our mind any part of our disposition or our actions that we still need to surrender to You. Give us the power to change and conform to Your standards. Help us to resist temptation, not only by giving us Your strength, but by showing us practically how we can distance ourselves from it. Help us to identify our particular areas of weakness so that we can surrender those to You. Lead us to the specific Scriptures we will need to counteract the enemy's attacks when they come. Arrange circumstances in our lives so that we can better follow You. Enable us to be self-controlled, composed, and godly women whose behavior always reflects You. In Jesus Holy name we pray, Amen.

Chapter 8

Created to be Pure

Train the young women...to be pure.
Titus 2:5 ESV

Pure – *hagnos* {Greek} – "Innocent, perfect, holy."

Purity is an important (and often overlooked) part of the life of a Christ-following woman. We were created to pursue a path that is set apart and pleasing to God. A Christian woman's life should be distinctly different than the lives of those who are not believers in Jesus. We will never do this perfectly, but our aim should be holiness.

For God has not called us for impurity, but in holiness.
1 Thessalonians 1:7 ESV

As obedient children, do not be conformed to the passions of your former ignorance, but as He who called you is holy, you also be holy in all your conduct, since it is written, "You shall be holy, for I am holy." 1 Peter 1:14-16 ESV

I know holiness can be a scary word. The last word I would have used to describe myself as a new Christian was holy. The concept of holiness seemed disconnected and unattainable. God was holy. Church was a holy place. I was not and could never be holy. I am so grateful that God, in His love and mercy, corrected my wrongly held belief. He showed me not only *could* I be holy, it was actually something He calls all of His followers to be.

I had fallen into the trap of faulty thinking that pervades much of the church culture today. Many claim to be Christians while they continue to pursue immorality and worldly passions. They attend church on Sunday and then forget about God for the rest of the week. They view God as holy, but do not pursue holiness in their personal lives and conduct. We should be careful not to fall into this snare. God cares deeply about how we live every day of the week. Not just on Sundays. He created us to be women who would pursue purity daily. In heart, thought, and action.

Only let your manner of life be worthy of the gospel of Christ. Philippians 2:27 ESV

Purity originates in our hearts and thoughts. So, what are we thinking about? Cultivating a pure heart means we refuse to entertain thoughts that are sinful or contrary to the will of God. We set our minds on thinking God-honoring thoughts.

Finally brothers, whatever is true, whatever is honorable, whatever is just, whatever is pure, whatever is lovely, whatever is commendable, if there is any excellence, if there is anything worthy of praise, think about these things. Philippians 4:8 ESV

As we all know from personal experience, controlling our thoughts does not come easily. One bad thought can spiral downward into a whirlwind of negativity. We must be able to quickly recognize critical, sinful, or pessimistic thoughts and intentionally replace them with God's truth. Give no consent to sinful thoughts.

Let's say I begin to have an angry thought about another person. I have two choices I can make. I can choose to nurture this thought and continue to think about all the ways I am upset with this person (by so-doing, dishonoring God and only upsetting myself further), or I can choose to replace the thought with a more loving and gracious one. I can ask God's forgiveness and petition for His help to redirect my thoughts. Another example would be replacing worrisome and doubtful thoughts with thoughts of God's provision and faithfulness. Refusing to give in to the temptation of these negative thoughts will keep us pure in heart. Purity of heart leads to purity of action.

Another step we can take to be proactive in purity is a careful inventory of what we allow into our spirits. This involves paying close attention to what we hear and see. We are a product of the books we read, the music we listen to, the programs we watch, and who we surround ourselves with. We may think these things are inconsequential, but the truth is they have a large impact on our lives. Remaining pure means we guard ourselves against outside influences that go against the word of God. Jesus' words here are so powerful:

"The eye is the lamp of the body. So if your eye is healthy, your whole body will be full of light, but if your eye is bad, your whole body will be full of darkness."
Matthew 6:22-23 ESV

We can keep our spiritual eyes healthy and full of light by making wise choices about entertainment and conversation. My rule of thumb is if I wouldn't feel comfortable watching, listening, or saying something with Jesus right next to me, I should remove myself from the situation. This means I sometimes have to make tough choices such as walking away from a conversation or leaving a movie that is glorifying sin. Truth is, we should never find entertainment in something that breaks God's heart. We were designed to be women who would hold fast to purity and honor God with every choice.

Let us pray these words of King David and keep our eyes pure!

Turn my eyes from looking at worthless {evil, deceptive, empty} things and give me life in your ways.
Psalm 119:37 ESV {emphasis mine}

I will set no wicked thing before my eyes. Psalm 101:3a ESV

One of the best examples of purity in Scripture is found in the story of Daniel. Daniel was a Jewish captive of the Babylonian empire. He was among those chosen to be assimilated into the Babylonian culture to ultimately serve King Nebuchadnezzar. He was to learn their language, religion, and culture. Through this service, Daniel would be rewarded greatly and the king's favor would be upon him. He would have treasures and pleasures forevermore.

The first temptation came when Daniel was presented non-kosher food to eat by the king's eunuch. He refused. He knew violating the dietary laws God had laid down for the Jewish people would pollute him and render him unclean. Daniel refused to betray the Lord and compromise the purity of his faith. This refusal showed where his loyalty lied.

God rewarded this decision by softening the eunuch's heart to allow Daniel to eat only vegetables. He still grew to be a strong and able servant, surprising everyone. Later in Daniel's story he refused to bow down to Nebuchadnezzar, which ultimately resulted in him being thrown into the lion's den. Again, the Lord rescued him. What was Daniel's secret to resisting temptation? We find the answer here :

But Daniel resolved that he would not defile himself with the king's food, or with the wine that he drank.
Daniel 1:8a ESV

Daniel resolved before any temptation came that he would not defile himself. He was committed and determined. He would remain pure, and his loyalty to the Lord would be steadfast. He said no to himself and, in so doing, said yes to God. The word resolved means to set in place. Daniel made a firm decision that he would remain innocent before the Lord. God rewarded his commitment with favor and compassion, giving Daniel strength, skill, and wisdom.

Our key to becoming women who stay pure is to make an unyielding decision that we will honor God in all of our choices, no matter what temptation comes our way. Our loyalty will be unshakeable. God's opinion will matter more than anyone's. We make this commitment out of love for Him and a desire to do what pleases Him.

We resolve to be :
Women of sexual purity.
Women who keep our promises.
Women of honesty and integrity.
Faithful wives and mothers.
Women of clean hearts and clean lips.

As we commit to living pure lives that honor God, the lives we were created to live, we will be greatly rewarded. The greatest of all these blessings will be the very presence of our Almighty Creator, with us always, from now into eternity.

Blessed are the pure in heart, for they shall see God.
Matthew 5:8 ESV

Personal Reflection:

Do my choices in entertainment nurture God's light in my heart, or do they sway me towards darkness? What changes can I make to honor God in this area?

Am I keeping my thoughts pure by choosing to meditate on God's word, and nurture thoughts that are lovely?

What kind of commitments can I make in my life to help me to stand firm in moments of temptation?

Heavenly Father, we long to be the women You created us to be. Women who are pure in heart and action. Help us to think thoughts that honor You and honor others. Help us to make the right decisions to keep our spirits pure. Keep our eyes from looking at worthless things. Convict us by Your Holy Spirit when we are participating in any activity that breaks your heart. Help us to love what You love and hate what You hate. Open our eyes to the spiritual battle around us and keep us sensitive to sin. Grow us daily and draw us ever closer to You. We pray our desire will be only to please You and to glorify you with our lives. Keep us innocent and pure and strengthen our resolve not to defile ourselves in any way. Reward us with the peace and joy that comes from knowing we are walking in Your will and bless us with Your glorious presence. In Jesus Majestic and Holy name we pray. Amen.

Chapter 9
Created to be a Homemaker

Train the young women to be…working at home.
Titus 2:5 ESV

She looks well to the ways of her household and does not eat
the bread of idleness. Proverbs 31:27 ESV

God places immense value on the home. For those of us who are wives and/or mothers, this is our highest calling. If this is not yet your season but you aspire to be a wife or mother someday, this will be your calling as well. Our homes ought to be places of beauty, comfort, and peace. They should be an oasis of light in an otherwise dark and chaotic world. It is in the home that our families are refreshed and comforted. It is there that our children are nurtured and nourished, mind body and soul. Home is where the heart is.

If we are seeking to honor God with our lives, we must recognize that the home is precious to Him. We should be intentional about filling our homes with love, laughter, and God's Word. There is no greater assignment in the life of a married woman than overseeing the affairs of her household. Home always comes first.

By wisdom a house is built and through understanding it is
established; through knowledge its rooms are filled with rare
and beautiful treasures. Proverbs 24:3-4 NIV

Some versions of the Bible use the phrase "keepers at home". I love this translation because it gives the notion of a woman who guards and cares for her dwelling. The keeper focuses her energy on the object to be kept. Nothing gets past the keeper, just as nothing will get past us when we diligently manage our homes. As women, we have the great privilege of setting the tones in our homes. We have the ability to establish the routine and arrange everything in such a way that our families are comfortable and cared for. What a blessing, and a great responsibility!

The wisest of women builds her house but folly with her own hands tears it down. Proverbs 14:1 ESV

The Bible speaks of two women in this passage, one wise and one foolish. The wise woman invests time into her home. She is a careful planner, resourceful, and her aim is to improve the life of her family. She builds her home and God is pleased. The foolish woman, on the other hand, is neglectful of her home life. She does not look to the affairs of her household. She may be careless, indulgent, or lazy when it comes to the home. This foolish woman may be busy with a number of other activities but if her home is neglected, God is not honored.

I was once this foolish woman. Busy, busy, always busy, but not prioritizing my home and family above all else. I was so distracted and consumed with other activities that I had forgotten the importance God places on the home. My family and my household duties were suffering at the expense of my other pursuits. It didn't matter that I was doing good deeds and helping people. What mattered was these tasks had overshadowed my most important assignment: my home. I am so grateful for the Lord's mercy and grace, which first convicted me, and then guided me to where I need to be.

"If you want to change the world, first go home and love your family." Mother Teresa

For me, this involved less time on social media and more focus on my family and my home. In an age where we can reach so many people, sometimes we neglect the ones that are right in front of us. It meant saying no to some of the endless demands of my time so I could prioritize my household. It meant making sure I left time each day in my busy schedule to clean so my husband could come home to a tidy house after a long day at work. Seemingly small adjustments. Yet these changes went a long way towards maintaining comfort and structure in my home. Focusing on my household and my family began to bring me so much joy. Helping my husband, nurturing my children, and making my home a place of love and beauty started to take precedence above all else, and along with that came the peace that comes with walking in God's will.

For each woman, prioritizing the home will look different. It may mean, as it did for me, putting down the phone and being present. It may mean giving yourself a to-do list every day of all those household tasks you have been putting off. Sometimes it means teaching yourself to cook so you can prepare wholesome meals for your family. It may even mean leaving the job consuming so much of your time that you can't focus on taking care of your home.

Whatever this will look like for you as you rearrange your life and priorities, prayerfully ask for God's help during the transition and He will abundantly provide. You will reap His blessings when you refocus your time and energy upon your home. I love this quote from Devi Titus, from her book *Home Experience: Making Your Home a Place of Love and Peace:*

"The reason our lives have become so confused and anxiety filled is that we have lost our focus on the worth and value God places on the home." *(Titus, 2011)*

This couldn't be truer. In a society where women are pressured to be more, do more, shatter the glass ceiling and have it all; the simple beauty of being a woman who stays home and cares for her family has been lost. The endless demands of our materialistic culture push women into the workforce and force them to put their children in the care of others. Infants and young children need their mothers. We were created to nurture them and strong bonds are formed in the early years. It is our responsibility to care for them and to teach them God's ways. We need to be present to set the foundation of their faith, for nothing is more important than this.

You shall love the Lord your God with all your heart and with all your soul and with all your might. And these words that I command you today shall be on your heart. You shall teach them diligently to your children, and shall talk of them when you sit in your house, and when you walk by the way, and when you lie down and when you rise. Deuteronomy 6:5-7 ESV

How can we diligently teach our children God's word if we are constantly away from our homes? We must be present to live out this command. This doesn't mean that working outside the home is forbidden, but it does mean the majority of a mother's time needs to be spent raising her children. It means our motives for working and for other time-consuming activities should be evaluated to make sure they are God-honoring.

If we are merely pursuing personal fulfillment or financial gain, at the expense of our families, we should consider how we can realign our lives to be in obedience to God's commands. Home first. Husband and children take precedence. If possible, careers can be put on hold while children are young. This may require sacrifice but remember, as Christ-followers we are asked to walk the narrow road of self-denial and obedience. We are told to put the needs of others, especially those of our families, above our own.

Do nothing from rivalry or conceit, but in humility count others more significant than yourselves. Let each of you look not only to his own interests, but also to the interests of others. Philippians 2:3-4 ESV

Sometimes the woman must be the sole breadwinner due to being single, or possibly a husband being injured. Sometimes, both parents must work just to make ends meet. In a perfect world there would be no sickness, no divorce, no struggling financially just to put food on the table. But we do not live in a perfect world; we await the perfection that comes in Heaven.

In these situations we do the best we can and work hard to maintain balance between all of our duties and responsibilities. We clear our schedules when outside of work so we can pour back into our families and care for our homes. We take time every day to teach our children about Jesus. We put Him at the center and maximize the time we do have with our families, by teaching them to love and obey His teachings. We trust that God's grace will carry us and empower us to do all things, even through difficult seasons.

As we begin to prioritize our homes above all else, we will see the fruit of that obedience flowing throughout our households. We will experience the immense peace that comes along with walking in God's will. And we will create an environment in which we, our husbands, and our children can truly thrive.

Personal Reflection:

Do I prioritize caring for my home and family above all else? Are there other, lesser pursuits, which are taking up too much of my time?

As I evaluate my hobbies and activities, am I pursuing these at the expense of time I could be devoting to my household? What can I do to rearrange my schedule so that my home takes precedence? If I work outside the home, do I take every opportunity while not working to be with my family and be a keeper of my home?

Is my reason for working outside of the home God-honoring? Do I place more value on money than I do on my family?

Heavenly Father, we recognize the importance You place on the home. As women who desire Your will to be lived out, we ask that You would reveal to us where we have fallen short in prioritizing our households. We thank You for Your beautiful Word, which convicts and guides, but never condemns. Thank You for the fresh hope and grace You constantly offer. Give us the desire to make our homes places of love, peace, and beauty. Strengthen us for whatever it is that You ask us to do. We acknowledge You as Provider and we know that our lives are in Your hands. We pray for You to specifically speak to each one of our situations, for we know they are all unique. Show us how we can better be obedient to everything You ask in this area. Give us wisdom to make the right choices and to be the best stewards of our time. Help us to leave behind hobbies or activities that are depriving our families from receiving our best. Show us specific ways in which we can go above and beyond to serve our families and care for our homes. We pray this over all wives and mothers and also those who aspire to be wives or mothers someday. Infuse us with Your grace and the strength to obey You in all things. In Jesus Holy name, Amen.

Chapter 10
Created to be Kind

Train the young women...to be kind.
Titus 2:5 ESV

The teaching of kindness is on her tongue.
Proverbs 31:26b ESV

We were designed to be women who would be known for our kindness. Goodness, patience, and forgiveness should mark our lives. When the Bible speaks of kindness, it isn't merely referring to the average nice person, but rather one who goes above and beyond to do good to others. Our kindness should not make sense. It should leave people scratching their heads and wondering what is different about us. The Greek word *chrestos* used for kindness in the New Testament meant useful, and willing to help. This is not a passive kindness.

We should seek out ways every day to be useful to other people. Intentional kindness goes out of the way for others. It constantly seeks to bring joy to another. This may come in the form of something small like an encouraging message to a friend, a compliment to a stranger, even a small gift for no reason. It can be smiling at people who walk by or holding the door for people to pass through. On a larger scale, it can be volunteering your time to help the homeless, or people in need in your community. Kindness can be exemplified in the way we choose to speak about others and the tone of our voice when we speak *to* others.

It can mean a gentle touch, a listening ear, or forgiveness and grace extended towards someone who has hurt us.

Put on then, as God's chosen ones, holy and beloved, compassionate hearts, kindness, humility, meekness and patience, bearing with one another and, if one has a complaint against another, forgiving each other; as the Lord has forgiven you, so you must also forgive. Colossians 3: 12-13 ESV

We have an amazing model of kindness in our Heavenly Father. God is love, and kindness is foundational to His character. He is a good, faithful, promise-keeping God. Slow to anger and abounding in steadfast love. His kindness doesn't sway with circumstances or mood. It is not dependent upon the object of His kindness (us), but rather it is a consistent aspect of His nature. As the recipients of God's kindness, we should be vigilant in extending it to others. As we meditate on the many verses that speak of God's kindness, we can better understand His character, and seek to emulate that character. Kindness is also a fruit of the Spirit which means the more time we spend with God, the more that fruit will be evident in our lives.

For His merciful kindness is great toward us; and the truth of the Lord endures forever. Praise the Lord! Psalm 117:2 NKJV

God expects us to go out of our way to bring His kindness to others. He calls us to be merciful and compassionate, loving our neighbor as ourselves. To give you an idea of the kindness we are to display, let's look at the parable Jesus told of the Good Samaritan. In the parable, a man was beaten, robbed, and left half-dead on the side of the road. Two men passed by and ignored the man before one finally stopped. This Good Samaritan went above and beyond to display kindness. Not only did he bandage the hurt man's wounds, he led him on his own animal to a nearby inn, and then paid for him to stay and recover. Each and every one of us has been created to live a life of intentional kindness, just like the man in this parable.

Exhibiting this type of kindness requires determination and sacrifice. It is a call to cultivate a lifestyle that will consistently personify love. A life that is willing to be interrupted for the sake of others.

And walk in the way of love, just as Christ loved us and gave Himself up for us as a fragrant offering and sacrifice to God.
Ephesians 5:2 NIV

Another way we can express kindness to others is through our willingness to forgive. Sometimes circumstances and emotions make it seem impossible to grant forgiveness. Yet it's important we strive to forgive no matter what the offense. We must do this not only to model kindness, but to be obedient to God and keep our own souls from becoming bitter. Holding on to the hurts others have caused us is like drinking poison and expecting the other person to die. It is a bitter pill that eats away at us from the inside. Jesus taught many times on forgiveness. He tells us to forgive not just seven times, but seventy times seven times. That's a lot of forgiveness! Scripture tells us when we refuse to forgive others; we ourselves will not be forgiven.

For if you forgive others their trespasses, your Heavenly Father will also forgive you, but if you do not forgive others their trespasses, neither will your Father forgive your trespasses. Matthew 6:14-15 ESV

It's important to note here that our salvation is not something we can earn. It is a free gift from God, only possible by the sacrifice of Jesus. Scriptures like this, if not interpreted within the broader context of the rest of the Bible, can be misunderstood to believe it is our actions (works) that save us. This is absolutely not the case. We are saved by grace and grace alone. However, as shown in this statement of Jesus and many others, a saved person will have a new Spirit which will enable him or her to live differently. Part of our new lives in Christ involves aligning ourselves to His will. Forgiveness is God's will for each and every one of us.

A downright refusal to forgive, and instead the choice to actively harbor bitterness and hold a grudge, can be evidence of a heart that is not fully surrendered to God. It can also be indicative of a person who does not fully know and understand God's grace. Someone who has experienced the magnificent love and grace of the Father will be eager to extend that same grace to others.

Be kind to one another, tenderhearted, forgiving one another, as God in Christ forgave you. Ephesians 4:32 ESV

Forgiving somebody does not mean what they did was okay. Their words or actions don't suddenly become justified. It sometimes may not even mean allowing them back into our lives. Forgiveness does mean we release that person from causing any more damage internally. It means realizing we are all human, with a flawed nature that is prone to making mistakes. People will hurt us, they will disappoint us, they will let us down.

Ultimately the battle we fight is not flesh and blood, but very spiritual in nature. The only one who will never hurt or disappoint us is Jesus, who has promised never to forsake us. Not one word of His will ever fail. No promise will ever be broken. He is our rock, our anchor, our trustworthy and never-changing Lord. He is the same yesterday, today, and forever.

Know therefore that the Lord your God is God, the faithful God who keeps covenant and steadfast love with those who love Him and keep his commandments, to a thousand generations. Deuteronomy 7:9 ESV

If you struggle with forgiving those who have hurt you please hear me; God sees you and He knows your heart. The fact that you struggle means you know it's not right to hold a grudge. You want to obey God, but it is difficult. There are situations in which we have been horribly hurt and deeply wounded. Understand God sees every tear and He can (and will) give the strength needed to truly let the offense go and forgive from the heart. He has promised to set everything right. He has promised to fight our battles. Vengeance is His and His alone. In these cases we should be honest with God. He already knows how we feel anyway. When we approach Him in prayer and tell Him we want to forgive but are struggling to get past what was done to us, He will help.

One of the best ways to cultivate forgiveness is to pray for those who have hurt you. Even if at first your prayers don't feel genuine, tell the Lord you want to be obedient and ask Him to change your heart. I can attest to the fact that, over time, He will!

I went through a heart-wrenching betrayal years ago. I lay awake night after night, rehearsing what had been done to me and wondering why. I wanted to forgive, but I just didn't know how to let it go. As time passed, and I continued to be obedient and pray for those who had hurt me, God changed my heart. At first, it was difficult to pray for them. I was still so angry and hurt. Yet, God took my willing heart and my obedience and He changed me through it. Soon, I realized I genuinely meant the prayers I was praying. And I sincerely desired goodwill toward my offenders.

When we contemplate the undeserved forgiveness God has lavished on us by sending His son to die a brutal death so we could be forgiven, this will help to put our grievances in perspective. No-one has possibly hurt us more than we have hurt God. We have sinned horribly against Him and broken His heart in so many ways. Yet, in His merciful kindness and infinite love, He forgives and redeems us, making peace with us by the cross.

But God, being rich in mercy, because of the great love with which He loved us, even when we were dead in our trespasses, made us alive together with Christ –by grace you have been saved – and raised us up with Him and seated us with Him in the heavenly places in Christ Jesus, so that in the coming ages He might show the immeasurable riches of His grace in kindness toward us in Christ Jesus. Ephesians 2:4-7 ESV

Another crucial facet of kindness is patience. Oh, patience. We are not a culture of patient people. We want what we want, the way we want it, and we want it right now! Patience is a virtue I constantly struggle with. I am prone to annoyance when others don't run on my time schedule and I get super frustrated when anything (or anyone) is not performing as efficiently as I would like. I hate being interrupted when I'm trying to focus on something.

The more I acknowledge my impatience for the sin that it is, the more I can cooperate with the Holy Spirit to eradicate impatience from my life. I do my part by acknowledging my impatient or unkind behavior and asking God (and others) for forgiveness. Then God does His part by helping me to be more patient and kind. I'm still a work in progress but I've made great improvements, with the help of the Holy Spirit.

With God's help, we can all become the women He created us to be. Women who exude patience, kindness, and mercy wherever we go. May we remember how patient the Lord is with us and purposefully and obediently exercise that same patience with others.

As we mirror the kindness of Jesus, our lives will speak volumes about His incredible mercy and love.

Be completely humble and gentle; be patient, bearing with one another in love. Ephesians 4:2 NIV

Personal Reflection:

Is there an area of my life where I am not exhibiting the kindness of Jesus? Am I treating every person that I encounter with love, dignity, and respect? Am I kind to my family?

Is there anyone currently or in my past with whom I am harboring bitterness or holding a grudge? Is there someone I need to extend forgiveness to? If so, how can I pray for this person and ask the Lord's help in letting go of the hurt that they have caused?

Is there anyone I need to apologize to, and ask forgiveness from?

What random acts of kindness can I plan to do today and in the future to uplift someone else?

Heavenly Father, we thank You so much for the undeserved kindness You have poured upon each one of us. We are so grateful for Your love and mercy. Thank You for Your unfailing Word. Thank You for always keeping Your promises to us. You are a good good Father. Help us to be kind and tenderhearted, compassionate and forgiving. Help us to model Your goodness wherever we go. We know kindness is contagious and one small act can set an avalanche of good deeds into motion. Bring people our way who need kindness the most. The angry, the hurting, those who feel as if no one will ever see or care. Help us to notice and to always do the next kind thing that You put in front of us. May our kindness consistently point to Jesus, and may we use kind acts as an opportunity to tell of His love. Help us to be quick to forgive those who have hurt us. Bring to mind any person we have not fully forgiven and help us to release that person from what they have done. We also ask that You would reveal to us any person we need to ask forgiveness from. Help us to be quick to admit our faults and smooth over conflicts. Give us the grace and strength to love even the unlovable. May our lives be marked with patience towards all. In Jesus Mighty name, Amen.

Chapter 11
Created in a Spiritual Order

Train the young women to...be submissive to their own husbands. Titus 2:5 ESV

If there is one word that makes women everywhere squirm, it is submission. This word bristles up again our sense of individuality and self-sufficiency. The word submit means to be subject to, or ranked in order. When I think of this concept, it does not conjure up the warm fuzzies. I think of harsh rulers and forced obedience at any cost. It does not help that the concept of submission has been twisted and viciously misused by individuals and throughout church history.

Abuse has been justified and tyranny has ensued in the name of submissiveness. Women have been made to feel inferior and without a voice. However, God's intent here is one of love. When we know God's heart, we know He always comes from a place of love and goodness. His commands are not burdensome and they are not meant to make us feel less-than or second class.

Women and men are uniquely different. A man cannot do everything a woman can do and a woman cannot do everything a man can do. And that's ok. We each have our own strengths and weaknesses. Yet, when we live as God directs, we see that God's perfect design is for men and women to complement one another. Where a husband is lacking, the wife compensates, and vice-versa. As we look at the biblical picture of a submissive wife, my prayer is that any misconceptions or hesitations you have about submission will be overcome with God's wisdom and grace. I just love this quote from John Piper about a wife's submissiveness:

"Submission is the divine calling of a wife to joyfully and fearlessly honor and affirm her husband's leadership and to help carry it through according to her gifts."
(The Beautiful Faith of Fearless Submission, April 15, 2007)

Submission is a divine calling and we have been appointed by God to serve Him in this manner. It is something we do out of reverence for Christ. We get the privilege of partnering with God as we live out this calling. The submissive wife is not one who timidly walks around on eggshells, bending to her husband's every whim, but rather she cheerfully recognizes and attests to his God-given role in the home. She knows the husband has been appointed by God to lead the family and this brings her much joy as she helps him carry out his God-given responsibilities to the best of her ability.

Wives submit to your own husbands, as to the Lord. For the husband is the head of the wife even as Christ is the head of the church, His body and is Himself, its Savior. Now as the church submits to Christ, so also wives should submit in everything to their husbands. Ephesians 5:22-24 ESV

Wives, submit to your own husbands as is fitting in the Lord. Husbands, love your wives and do not be harsh with them. Children, obey your parents in everything for this pleases the Lord. Colossians 3:18-21 ESV

These commands were given to the churches at Ephesus and Colossae, and their timeless truths are still applicable to women today. We can deepen our understanding of the concept of godly submission by looking at the other issues Paul addresses. In the preceding Scriptures, we see Paul painting a beautiful picture of a believer's new life in Christ. He stresses putting off the old life with its evil practices, (anger, theft, slander, filthy language, immorality) and putting on the new life in Christ. This new life is marked by kindness, forgiveness, thanksgiving, and reverence for God. He tells us:

For at one time you were darkness, but now you are light in the Lord. Walk as children of light (for the fruit of light is found in all that is good and right and true), and try to discern what is pleasing to the Lord. Ephesians 5:8-10 ESV

If then you have been raised with Christ, seek the things that are above, where Christ is, seated at the right hand of God. Set your minds on things that are above, not on things that are on earth. Colossians 3: 1-2 ESV

He then goes on to tell wives to be submissive to their husbands. He follows this with instructions for husbands to love their wives and children to obey their parents. He concludes with these lovely Scriptures, reminding us who we are truly serving:

Not by the way of eye-service, as people-pleasers, but as bondservants of Christ, doing the will of God from the heart, rendering service with a good will as to the Lord and not to man, knowing that whatever good one does, this he will receive back from the Lord. Ephesians 6:6-8a ESV

Whatever you do, work heartily, as for the Lord and not for men, knowing that from the Lord you will receive the inheritance as your reward. You are serving the Lord Christ. Colossians 3:23-24 ESV

So how can we look at submission differently now that we have all of this information? We see that God intends for His people to display good and righteous behavior. This behavior honors Christ. We see He loves us and desires for us to walk in the light, which will always be His perfect will for us. We are told to set our minds above, and seek to please God and God alone. We see that the spiritual order that He appointed (1. Husband 2. Wife 3. Child) is reflective of Christ and the church. We know God is our Creator and life works best when we follow His plan. Therefore, we can conclude that a family where the spiritual authority flows as God intended is a strong family. This family will be united, and it will function as God intended. It will stand strong against the schemes of the enemy.

For we do not wrestle against flesh and blood, but against the rulers, against the authorities, against the cosmic powers over this present darkness, against the spiritual forces of evil in the heavenly places. Ephesians 6:12 ESV

Satan, the enemy of our souls, knows that disrupting God's spiritual order will bring destruction and chaos to the home. He works very hard to undermine the male's role, and to make submission look so unattractive to the female that she will refuse to believe it is God's will for her life. He whispers in our ears that we must assert our independence, we must take charge. He tries to convince us that our husbands are completely incapable of leading the home.

This sneaky plan of his goes all the way back to the garden when the serpent whispered in Eve's ear, "Did God really say not to eat the fruit?" Eve took the bait and ate the forbidden fruit as her husband stood by and watched. Imagine the radically different outcome if Eve would have deferred to Adam on this life-altering decision and Adam would've wisely used his authority to send the devil packing. Not today Satan.

In this same way, when we are living in obedience to the chain of authority God has breathed out all over Scripture, we will be fortified against the attacks of the enemy. There will be no chinks in our families' armor when the godly husband submits to the Father, we submit to the husband, and the children submit to the parents. On the contrary, when we do not submit to God's desired order in the family, we give the devil a foothold into our lives.

Submit yourselves therefore to God. Resist the devil and he will flee from you. James 4:7 ESV

All of this being said let me just be real and say that submission is not always easy. I came to faith during my marriage, and at the time of initially writing this chapter my husband is still not following Christ (more on that later). Because of this, I have my own unique situation with many hurdles. Nevertheless; I am still responsible to be submissive to my husband. I still have to choose daily to honor Christ by submitting to the authority He has placed in my life.

Let me give you a few scenarios of how this plays out. Scene 1: We have an important decision to make as a family. I lovingly and wisely share my input with my husband but I let him know that the decision is ultimately his and I will support and honor his choice. Scene 2: I have my evening all planned out the way I want it to go but my husband expresses a desire to do something differently. I change my plans to appease him, rather than argue and fight to get my way or just flat out go against his wishes. Scene 3: My husband asks me specifically not to do something and even though I really want to, or I think it's a wise choice, I respect his request. I choose to let him lead because I know this is God's will. (The only exception to these is if my husband asks me to sin, I must respectfully disobey to stay in obedience to God.)

Does this mean I'm a doormat? Absolutely not. Does this mean I always agree? Not in the slightest. I can give my advice and express my opinion in a respectful way yet still give my husband the freedom to be the head of the family.

But I want you to understand that the head of every man is Christ, and the head of a wife is her husband, and the head of Christ is God. 1 Corinthians 11:3 ESV

One other important point on the topic of submission: submission never justifies abuse. If you are in a situation where you or your children are in an unsafe environment or being abused, please seek godly counsel and help from the authorities if necessary. It is never ok for a woman to be abused in the name of "submission".

God's design is for a man to love and honor his wife, and for a woman to submit to the man's leadership. Submission is a choice we make out of love and respect for Christ, not something that should be imposed upon us in a harmful way. God's intention is not for women to suffer under the hands of a tyrannical abuser who twists Scripture to justify his sinful behavior. A man is called to treat his wife with love and tender care.

Husbands, love your wives, just as Christ loved the church and gave himself up for her to make her holy, cleansing her by the washing with water through the word, and to present her to himself as a radiant church, without stain or wrinkle or any other blemish, but holy and blameless. In this same way, husbands ought to love their wives as their own bodies. He who loves his wife loves himself. Ephesians 5:25-28 NIV

Every time we choose to submit to our husbands, we choose submission to God. As our obedience grows in this area we will see the pleasant fruits of that obedience flowing all throughout our families. As we set our minds to honor and respect our husbands' roles in the home, our marriages will begin to thrive. Our homes will overflow with peace and joy. As we model a godly marriage for our children to see, we will set a beautiful example for them to follow in the future. God's favor will be upon our families as we honor His design for marriage. Our families will be strong, fortified against attack, and a beautiful reflection of our Lord and Savior, Jesus Christ.

Personal Reflection:
Do I tend to view submission as something negative? Am I afraid if I am submissive to my husband that he will not lead the family properly? If so, am I willing to let go of my beliefs and preconceived notions and trust God to ultimately lead my husband in the right direction?

Would I consider myself submissive to my husband? Would he say that I am a submissive wife?

Is there a particular area in my life where I am not submitting to my husband? How can I commit to living as God directs in this area?

Heavenly Father, we praise You and thank You for Your wisdom in creating the order of authority. As our Creator, You know best! Thank You for giving us softened hearts and opened minds to receive this message today. We pray to be doers of the word and not just hearers. We ask forgiveness for the times we have been disobedient to your design. We ask for Your Holy Spirit to fill us and give us the strength to always obey, no matter how difficult. We pray for each and every one of our husbands to stand in the authority You have given them over their families. We pray above all else, they will seek You first. We pray for these men to have strong relationships with You so they can lead their families with wisdom, truth, and grace. We cancel out every scheme and plan of the enemy to come against these men and attack the spiritual order You designed. We pray for firm, strong families where the husband submits to You, the wife submits to the husband, and the children obey the parents. We also pray for women being abused in the name of submission. We pray Your protection over them and Your comfort and guidance to remove themselves from unsafe environments and seek help. We pray You will lead the abusers into repentance and transformation. We ask that Your will be done in every single family praying this prayer today. In Jesus Holy and Precious name, Amen.

Chapter 12
Created to be an Excellent Wife

An excellent wife who can find? She is far more precious than jewels. The heart of her husband trusts in her, and he will have no lack of gain. She does him good, and not harm, all the days of her life. Proverbs 31:10-12 ESV

Her husband is known in the gates when he sits among the elders of the land. Proverbs 31:23 ESV

Excellence: Something of the highest quality. Biblically speaking: a woman of virtuous character, high morals, and strength.

God's will for you, whether you are married or aspiring to be a wife someday in the future, is to be an excellent wife. Before we delve into the practical application of being an excellent wife, let's go all the way back to Genesis for a deeper understanding of why we were created. Knowing God's intent for us, from the beginning of time, will help us to view our role as wives as the beautiful assignment that our Heavenly Father designed it to be.

In the beginning, God created. He created the moon and the sun, the land and the water, every plant to flourish in its season, and every animal that roamed the earth. He created all the beauty of nature and said that it was very good. After this He created Adam, the first human, from the dust of the ground. As God breathed into Adam's nostrils, life began for him. And it was good.

Yet, Adam was alone. As God contemplated how each animal had a partner, He realized there was no helper for Adam.

Then the Lord God said, "It is not good that the man should be alone; I will make him a helper fit for him." .... So the Lord God caused a deep sleep to fall upon the man, and while he slept took one of his ribs and closed up its place with flesh. And the rib that the Lord God had taken from the man he made into a woman and brought her to the man. Then the man said, "This at last is bone of my bones and flesh of my flesh; she shall be called Woman, because she was taken out of Man." Therefore a man shall leave his father and his mother and hold fast to his wife, and they shall become one flesh.
Genesis 2:18, 2:21-24 ESV

We were created to be helpers to our husbands. To partner with them in life and ease the burdens they carry. To encourage them, uplift them, and care for their needs. We were designed to be their helpers, their companions, their life partners. A husband should value his wife as more precious than jewels because of her excellence. One of God's greatest gifts to us is marriage. Marriage is a beautiful depiction of how Christ relates to the church and when we have healthy, properly functioning marriages, they can point others to Him. God's design for marriage is for each partner to equally respect, value, and love each other. Together, we are to be united and harmonious. Yet, because we were built with different characteristics, we will each fulfill different roles.

Men were created to provide, to protect, and to lead the family. They are strong, adventurous, and practical. Women were created to nurture, to love, to build relationships and bring peace. They are tender-hearted, thoughtful, and intuitive. These characteristics complement each other wonderfully to create the perfect union. Men and women were also created uniquely and distinctly to reflect God's character.

We each personify different aspects of God's personality, for both men and women were created in His image.

So God created man in his own image, in the image of God He created them, male and female He created them.
Genesis 1:27 ESV

And {we} have put on the new self, which is being renewed in knowledge after the image of its Creator. Colossians 3:10 ESV

When we take our role as wives seriously, and grow to be the excellent wife Scripture speaks of, we bring honor to God. So what is an excellent wife, biblically speaking? We can refer to the Scriptures at the beginning of this chapter to find our first clues. First, an excellent wife is trustworthy. She is loyal and can be counted on for support and to hold up her end of the work. Her husband can trust that she will manage the home and take care of his needs. He can trust her in all things. With the home, with the finances, with his heart.

The excellent wife does good to her husband at all times. She doesn't speak badly about her husband to others. She is concerned about preserving his reputation amongst everyone. He is well-respected in the community, partially due to the upstanding behavior of his wife. She holds him in high regard, and with utmost respect.

However, let each one of you love his wife as himself, and let the wife see that she respects her husband. Ephesians 5:33 ESV

Men need to feel honored by their wives. It's the way they were wired. Women typically respond better to love, while men crave respect. This is a foundational truth about men that we may not understand as women, but we need to get deep down into our souls. When a man feels disrespected it attacks him to the very core of his character. This leads us to ask ourselves some tough questions. Do our husbands feel respected by us? Do we put them down in public, talk over them, or otherwise shame them? We may inadvertently do this without even realizing it. We need to be conscious of our attitude towards our husbands. Does the way we talk about them when they aren't around convey that we respect them? It's so tempting to want to vent our frustrations about our husbands to others. I know I have been guilty of this. Yet, in most cases (unless we are truly seeking godly advice and prayer), it is better to go directly to God with our frustrations.

When we take issues with our husbands to God rather than complaining to others, multiple things happen. 1. We maintain an attitude of respect towards our husbands and preserve their reputations. 2. We have peace because we didn't gossip or complain to others. 3. We partner with God who will be the true agent of change in our husbands. All the nagging in the world will not change the things we don't like about them. Trust me, I've tried. It's always best to go to God and ask Him to work on our husbands' hearts rather than complaining to others or trying to change them on our own.

An excellent wife is the crown of her husband, but she who causes shame is like rottenness in his bones.
Proverbs 12:4 NKJV

Other ways we can respect our husbands are not purposely doing things we know bother them, and giving them our full attention when they speak. Nothing is more disrespectful than looking at our phones or being distracted when our husbands (or anyone) are talking to us. In the age of smart-phones and extreme multitasking, this may be hard to do. Yet the call to excellence means we make an intentional choice to put down whatever we are doing and give our husbands the respect they deserve when they talk. This goes a long way towards making them feel special and appreciated.

Another way we can excel at being a wife is to have the home as a place of order and peace when our husbands come home from work. Most men come home from a long day of work exhausted and hungry. They don't want to come home to a messy house full of chaos. With some extra effort and intentionality, we can make sure they have a warm welcome when they return home. We can have the house picked up, and dinner either ready or cooking. We can have ourselves prepared and the children ready and excited to see Daddy.

Friends, I know there are days this is tough to do. Please know that sometimes you will have a rough day and it's just not attainable. Give yourself grace. These words are not meant to make you feel guilty about not measuring up. They are meant to be a guideline and a biblical goal to set for yourself in order to go above and beyond for your husband and be the excellent wife God has called you to be.

It is helpful to start planning for this about an hour before our husbands come home. The kiddos can be a huge help in this area. It takes just a little planning and intentionality, and maybe some rearranging of schedules. I ask my four year old for help cleaning up and tell him we are getting ready so Daddy can come home to a nice clean home. We prepare dinner together if he's feeling up for helping.

I also try to remember to fix my makeup and make sure I look at least halfway decent. Or at the very least get out of my pajamas and brush my teeth. (We all have those days right?) Men are very visual and it will help keep the romance alive if we put effort into this. He will be so appreciative and glad to be home. He will rave about what an excellent wife he has!

Your wife will be like a fruitful vine within your house; your children will be like olive shoots around your table.
Psalm 128:3 ESV

Vines and olives were frequently used in Hebrew poetry to symbolize fruitfulness and a happy, flourishing state. The wife who thoughtfully prepares and plans for her husband will flourish. Her children will be happy and fruitful. And while we're on the subject of children, there is no better way to end a discussion on being an excellent wife than talking about the birds and the bees. The Bible says we should not deprive each other physically. Intimacy is an important part of a marriage and a flourishing sex life makes a husband very happy indeed. In fact, research shows that men feel the closest to their wives during sex. On the flip side, repeated rejection in this area cuts them deeply, and stirs up feelings of worthlessness and inadequacy.

We all know how easy it is to let this part of our marriage sit on the back burner. Personally, I don't always feel up to this task. At the end of the day, I am worn out and tired and just want to sit down and rest for a few minutes. After being nagged, pulled on, and whined at all day I need a little space. If you have small children, I know you can relate! Yet, I know my husband needs my love and affection too. I confess too many times he gets my leftovers.

It takes a conscious effort and commitment to just say yes. Sex makes him happy, content, and fulfilled. And I don't ever regret it either (wink, wink). It is crucial to keep this part of our marriages alive and thriving. If we are having intimacy issues, we should seek the Lord's guidance on how to overcome. We should ask Him not only to renew our desires to please our husbands in this way, but to heal any wounds that are keeping us from delighting in this part of our marriages. God created sex as a divine gift for marriage, and His will is for both partners to enjoy the deep connection that comes from it. It is a beautiful union of mind, body, and soul.

The husband should give to his wife her conjugal rights, and likewise the wife to her husband. For the wife does not have authority over her own body, but the husband does. Likewise the husband does not have authority over his own body, but the wife does. Do not deprive one another...
1 Corinthians 7:3-5a ESV

Living up to the biblical definition of an excellent wife may seem like a daunting task. However, with knowledge, dedication (and most importantly the help of the Holy Spirit along the way), we can accomplish anything God asks of us. The examples I gave are lessons God has taught me over the years. I wasn't always the wife I am today. I take no credit for the improvements I have made in this area. It is only by seeking God's will, reading His Word and (by His grace) applying it to my life that I am who I am now.

I thank Him I'm not who I used to be. Yet I know there is always room to improve, and the lessons will keep on coming. He has consistently grown me as a wife and my relationship with my husband is thriving because of it. I know yours will too! Moving forward, let us all continue to ask the Lord daily how we can exceed our husbands' expectations and bring them joy. This is the key to a great marriage, and a crucial component to becoming the excellent wives God created us to be!

Personal Reflection:
How can I commit to becoming an excellent wife? Am I willing to ask my husband where i can improve and how I can be a better helper to him?

Am I respectful to my husband? How do I speak about him to others? What can I change in the way I act or speak to consistently convey a respectful attitude?

When my husband returns from work does he return home to chaos or peace? Do I have dinner ready for him and everyone prepared for his arrival? How can I rearrange my schedule to plan a warm welcome for him when he comes home? If I work, how can I prepare beforehand so he can still feel appreciated, loved, and cared for? (A crock-pot works wonders for these situations.)

Heavenly Father, we thank You for Your beautiful design of men and women. You made us uniquely different, yet we fit together so perfectly. Thank You for the beauty of marriage. You have given us such an amazing gift of love and companionship. Help us to become the excellent wives You created us to be. May we be helpers to our husbands. May they be able to trust in us, count on us, and lean on us. May we always respect them and care for them. Forgive us for the times we have forsaken this most precious assignment. Shower us with Your grace and empower us to be all You created us to be. Show us ways in which we can please our husbands and bring them joy. Give us the strength and energy to go the extra mile for them. We pray for strong, united, and harmonious marriages that point to You. We pray for those who aren't yet wives, that You would bring good, godly husbands into their lives. We pray for those who are widows, that You would comfort them, and surround them with your love. We pray for those who choose to remain single, that You would bless them with undivided devotion towards You, and holiness in mind, body, and spirit. Above all, we pray Your will be done in every single life and every single home represented here. In Jesus beautiful name we pray, Amen.

Chapter 13

Created to Work

She perceives that her merchandise is profitable. Her lamp does not go out at night. She puts her hands to the distaff, and her hands hold the spindle. Proverbs 31:18-19 ESV

She seeks wool and flax and works with willing hands. She is like the ships of the merchant; she brings her food from afar. Proverbs 31: 13-14

Work –*Asah* – "Accomplish. Achieve. Acquire. This Hebrew word conveys the central notion of performing an activity with a distinct purpose, a moral obligation, or goal in view."

Willing – *Chephets {Hebrew}* – "The delight of hands in their labor."

God calls us women, whoever we are and whatever season we are in, to put Him at the center of our lives and do everything for His glory. We are chosen and appointed by Him to work hard and to give our absolute best to every assignment. We can turn even the smallest and most mundane of tasks into an opportunity to glorify Him!

When we keep the goal in view of pleasing Christ, no endeavor is wasted. We honor our Creator when we go about housework with a cheerful heart and a mindset eager to bless our families. Faithful dedication to our ministries or careers brings Him glory. Joyful perseverance through difficult duties pleases Him. We should do our best at whatever work He brings our way, keeping in mind that God values and blesses hard-working women.

Therefore, my beloved brothers, be steadfast, immovable, always abounding in the work of the Lord, knowing that in the Lord your labor is not in vain. 1 Corinthians 15:58 ESV

Doing our work, not begrudgingly, but with an "I get to" attitude also brings God much glory. This was a lesson I learned not long ago, as a frazzled, stressed-out mama. As I mentally went over the list of all the things I needed to do before I could finally go to bed one evening, God revealed something profound to me. How often I had gone through my days allowing the devil to steal my joy. How often I had allowed my to-do list and my busyness to frustrate and exhaust me, rather than being joyful at the opportunities to serve my loved ones. I was certainly not working with willing hands, hands that delighted in their labor. Hurrying from one activity to the next, thinking about all the work I still needed to accomplish, had left me irritated and exhausted. It dawned on me that I needed a new perspective.

This is the day that the Lord has made; let us rejoice and be glad in it. Psalm 118:24 ESV

Scripture says to render all of our work to the Lord, as a service to Him. The Bible tells us to enjoy each day, because truly each day is a gift. I realized I could shift my perspective by changing my "I have to's" to "I get to's". Being overwhelmed that I had a ton of dishes to wash could change to thanking God I am able to feed my family three delicious home-cooked meals every day. Being stressed out because I had a messy house that needed cleaning could switch to being grateful I had a roof over my head and a place to create beautiful memories with my family. Annoyance that my toddler absolutely would not fall asleep without me could instead create an opportunity for me to enjoy those extra snuggles that will not last forever. Each one of those obligations could be turned into an opportunity to praise God and to delight in my work. Having a grateful heart that praises and blesses God truly changes everything.

A joyful heart is good medicine, but a crushed spirit dries up the bones. Proverbs 17:22 ESV

Our attitude is vital as we look at the work set before us. Will we complete our work with a crushed, angry spirit or will we be joyful and thankful? The choice is ours. One choice will honor God and bring peace to our hearts, the other choice will not. Our circumstances and the work we have to do most likely will not change; but we have the power to bring the light and love of Jesus to every activity. As we work hard and delight in our labor, God is glorified. When we keep a grateful heart as we go about our work, we make much of His name.

Do all things without grumbling or disputing, that you may be blameless and innocent, children of God without blemish in the midst of a crooked and twisted generation, among whom you shine as lights in the world. Philippians 2:14-15a ESV

Sometimes the amount of work we have is overwhelming. Even setting about our tasks with a joyful attitude can't always counteract the fact that, as women, we have a lot on our plates. We wear multiple hats, and have many responsibilities. One amazing piece of advice I learned helps to maintain balance in my life. I know it will be helpful in yours as well.

Imagine yourself as a juggler. All of the responsibilities you have in your life are the balls. So, for example: I have a mom ball, a wife ball, a writing ball, a laundry ball, cleaning ball, etc, etc. Every day we are going to drop a ball. It just isn't possible to keep all of them up, all of the time. We need to give ourselves grace when this happens. Yet, the key is, never let the same ball drop two days in a row. So simple, yet so life-changing! I try to remind myself of this often. It helps me to stay on track and keeps everything flowing smoothly in the household.

Aside from our usual day-to-day responsibilities, we must keep in mind the greater mission for each and every one of us, as co-laborers in God's kingdom. As Daughters of the Most High God, we are given some of the most meaningful work here on this Earth. Our God-given assignments can bring us much joy, and fulfill us like nothing else, as we seek His purpose for us daily. Every day is a new adventure, prepared in advance for us by the Father. We were created on purpose and for a purpose!

For we are His workmanship, created in Christ Jesus for good works, which God prepared beforehand, that we should walk in them. Ephesians 2:10 ESV

Every day God places us exactly where He wants us, so that His plans will go forth. He intricately designs every detail and arranges our circumstances in such a way that His will is accomplished. Before we have devised our own plans for the day, the Lord has established His. Our job is to be faithful to each task He sets before us: whether we are working hard in our homes for our families, faithfully serving in ministry or jobs outside of the home, or encouraging and speaking truth to others. As we listen for His still small voice, He will guide us. We were created to live each day for Jesus. This brings Him much glory.

Many are the plans in the mind of a man, but it is the purpose of the Lord that will stand. Proverbs 19:21 ESV

We have each been uniquely designed by our Creator with very specific skills that He intends for us to use to glorify Him and to build up His church. Every one of us has a unique niche in God's kingdom that only we can fill. He gifts us in many ways individually, to benefit us all as a whole. Once we determine our gifts and specific function in the body of Christ, we can work diligently in those areas to bring God glory. Some have been given the gift of teaching; some the gift of encouragement, some excel in acts of service. These are merely a few of the talents the Lord has instilled in His people.

Having gifts that differ according to the grace given to us, let us use them; if prophecy, in proportion to our faith; if service, in our serving; the one who teaches, in his teaching; the one who exhorts, in his exhortation; the one who leads, ,with zeal; the one who does acts of mercy, with cheerfulness. Romans 12:6-8 ESV

It is vital for us to seek God's wisdom on our specific gifts and place in His Kingdom. A life that does not fulfill the purpose for which God has created it is a wasted life. Jesus told a parable of three men who were entrusted by their master with a specific amount of talents, each according to their ability. Two of the men faithfully invested their talents and had much to show to the master when he returned. To these the master said "Well done, good and faithful servant. You have been faithful over a little; I will set you over much" (Matthew 25:23).

The third man buried his talent in the ground and had nothing to show his master when he returned. He was scolded and what talent he did have was taken away and given to the other faithful servants. My prayer for myself and for you, Dear Reader, is that we won't be women who bury our God-given talents. Rather, we will be women who discover our niche in His kingdom and work hard for His glory. When we do this, we can look forward to one day hearing these beautiful words from the lips of Jesus: "Well done, good and faithful servant, enter into the joy of your master" (Matthew 25:23).

No matter who you are, where you are, or how far you feel you may have wandered from God's plan; if you are reading this God has a purpose for you! No life is insignificant to Him. If there is breath in your lungs, then you have not yet completed His mission for you on this Earth. You can begin seeking Him and asking for Him to reveal to you your specific set of gifts and the calling He has placed on your life. He will always answer the prayers of a heart that desires to do His will. Once your calling is revealed and you begin to passionately pursue your unique role on this Earth, working hard at whatever the Lord brings your way, joy and purpose will mark your life, and God's kingdom will advance. Remember that you are chosen by God and pre-destined for His kingdom purposes. Let that set your soul on fire as you fervently seek His will for your life!

Personal Reflection:
Am I working diligently at every task the Lord has given me in this season of my life? Is my attitude joy-filled and eager to bless those around me or am I irritated and angry when I go about my daily tasks? How can I realign my perspective so as to have a merry heart and to honor God?

Am I placing unrealistic expectations upon myself when it comes to my workload? How can I adjust my expectations and my schedule to be less overwhelming?

Do I know the specific calling that God has placed on my life? What skills has He gifted me with that I can use to build up His church? How can I glorify Him and be faithful with the talents I have been given?

Heavenly Father, we praise You that we are fearfully and wonderfully made! You have created each of us with a distinct purpose and role to fill and we pray You will make our unique callings known to us. We want to see You glorified in our lives and we want to see Your kingdom advance. Your will be done, on Earth as it is in heaven. Reveal our gifts to us and help us to use those gifts for Your glory and for the good of Your church. We pray that whatever tasks You set before us we will complete with hard work and joyful perseverance. Help us to balance our responsibilities and to give ourselves grace when we feel like we have dropped the ball. Help us to cultivate merry hearts, whether we are serving others on the mission field, or simply doing laundry and washing dishes. May every task be an opportunity for us to honor You. We know You are honored when we work hard and when our attitude glorifies You. Help us to keep You always in our minds and close to our hearts. In Jesus name, Amen

Chapter 14
Created to Serve

She rises while it is yet night and provides food for her household and portions for her maidens. Proverbs 31:15 ESV

The proverbs 31 woman has the heart of a servant. Not only does she forsake precious sleep to rise early and prepare food for her family, she is also thoughtful and considerate enough to provide food for her maidens. A maiden in biblical times was a female servant. How ironic that this woman was serving her own servants! This is such a beautiful image of the life we were created to live. Not to be served, but serve. To consider the needs of someone else even before our own. To go above and beyond in acts of service and selflessly give all that we have for the betterment of others. This is what counts the most in God's Kingdom: in humility and love, putting others first.

Let the greatest among you be your servant. Whoever exalts himself will be humbled, and whoever humbles himself will be exalted. Matthew 23:11-12 ESV

What better example for us to follow as we pursue the servant life than that of Jesus Himself. Jesus was always pouring Himself out for the people around Him. He was so compassionate, constantly prioritizing the needs of others above His own. We forget that, though Jesus was fully God, He was also fully man. He had physical needs just as we do. He became tired. He felt hunger. He experienced every single emotion we do. Yet in the Scriptures we constantly see Him teaching, healing, and loving the people around Him. He did this whether He was tired, hungry, or even grieved. A great depiction of this is found in Matthew's account of the gospel.

{King Herod} sent and had John {the Baptist} beheaded in the prison, and his head was brought on a platter and given to the girl, and she brought it to her mother. And his disciples came and took the body and buried it, and they went and told Jesus. Now when Jesus heard this, He withdrew from there in a boat to a desolate place by Himself. But when the crowds heard it, they followed Him on foot from the towns. When He went ashore He saw a great crowd and He had compassion on them and healed their sick. Matthew 14: 10-14 ESV

John the Baptist and Jesus literally knew each other since being in the womb. The Scriptures say John leaped for joy in his mother's belly when Mary, pregnant with Jesus, came near. They grew up together as cousins, and I can imagine shared a very special bond. After hearing of His loved one's death, Jesus needed to be by Himself to mourn, and most likely have solitude prayer time with the Father. Yet, the crowds followed. Jesus saw the multitude of desperate people who needed His help and, instead of prioritizing His own needs, He had compassion and put Himself on the back burner to care for the people. Jesus did not come to be served, but to serve. These are His own words to His disciples:

"But whoever would be great among you must be your servant, and whoever would be first among you must be your slave, even as the Son of Man came not to be served, but to serve, and to give His life as a ransom for many."
Matthew 20:26b-27 ESV

Part of becoming the women God created us to be involves imitating Jesus by looking for opportunities to serve those God has placed in our lives. Whether the people in our sphere of influence are numerous or few, there is always someone to serve. We can serve our families by valuing their needs above our own. We can take the time to reach out to someone who is hurting. We can serve the homeless, volunteer to fill a need, or look for a place to serve within our local church. Any act of service can be done for God's glory. As we choose to put aside our own wants and focus on serving others, we will experience many blessings God has for us. It is truly better to give than to receive.

In all things I have shown you that by working hard in this way we must help the weak and remember the words of the Lord Jesus, how He Himself said, "It is more blessed to give than to receive." Acts 20:35 ESV

One of the most beautiful depictions of servant-hood is found in the gospel of John as he recounts the time when Jesus washed the disciples' feet. First Jesus prepared the items He would need to complete His task. Then Jesus knelt and began washing the feet of His disciples. As He came to Peter, Peter was astonished! "Lord!" he says. "Do you wash my feet?" I imagine Peter was thinking, "Wait a minute! This should be the other way around!" Yet Jesus, true to character, kindly and directly explained why the washing was absolutely necessary. After finishing, Jesus reminded His disciples to do the same for one another.

When He had washed their feet and put on His outer garments and resumed His place, he said to them, "Do you understand what I have done to you? You call me Teacher and Lord, and you are right, for so I am. If I then, your Lord and Teacher, have washed your feet, you also ought to wash one another's feet. For I have given you an example that you also should do just as I have done to you. Truly, truly, I say to you, a servant is not greater than his master, nor is a messenger greater than the one who sent him. If you know these things, blessed are you if you do them." John 13:12-17 ESV

A woman with the heart of a servant will find great joy not just in hearing about the selfless way Jesus lived His life, but in pursuing that same lifestyle for herself. She will give with no expectation of her generosity being returned. She will purposefully seek out those who can never repay her, and lavish God's goodness upon them. In a culture that is very self-absorbed, a woman who selflessly gives in this way will stand out. As we pursue this type of lifestyle, our lives will point to Jesus and confirm our faith, thereby bringing God much glory!

So what do we do when our serving goes unnoticed or we think our generosity is being taken for granted? I know how frustrating it can be to feel underappreciated or taken advantage of. In these instances, we really have to be intentional about giving our frustrations to God and praying for Him to change our hearts and expectations. He will be faithful to switch our focus to pleasing Him even if no one else seems to notice.

Those little extras we do around the house to please our husbands? God sees. The effort we put into hospitality so others will feel comfortable in our homes? God notices. Every step we take to place the needs of someone else above our own is recognized and appreciated by our Heavenly Father. Every burden we bear for another will be rewarded, whether in this life or the next. Most importantly, when we serve others, we are fulfilling God's purpose for our lives and with that always comes great joy!

For God is not unjust so as to overlook your work and the love that you have shown for His name in serving the saints, and you still do. Hebrews 6:10 ESV

And let us not grow weary of doing good, for in due season we will reap, if we do not give up. So then, as we have opportunity, let us do good to everyone, and especially to those who are of the household of faith. Galatians 6:9-10 ESV

Personal Reflection:
Is my focus mainly on how I can gratify my own desires, or do I seek out ways I can do for others? Do I give with no expectations of my kindness being returned?

What is one thing I can do today to go above and beyond to serve those that God has placed in my life?

How can I volunteer my time and talents to serve others outside my sphere of influence, or to fill a need at my church?

Heavenly Father, we pray today that we will lay aside our own wants and desires to be in service to someone else. We ask for the help of the Holy Spirit to cultivate the heart of a servant. We know Jesus came not to be served, but rather to serve. Help us to be like Him. To reflect His love in how we treat those around us. Make us quick to recognize and meet the needs of the people You have placed in our lives. Fill us up with Your kindness, love, humility, and goodwill, so we can overflow those attributes to everyone we come in contact with. May our focus always be pleasing You. Let us not seek affirmation from those we serve, rather, remind us that when we live in obedience to You in this way, we will be abundantly blessed. Show us specific ways we can serve those in our lives and help us to live this out every day in every way. In Jesus mighty name, Amen.

Chapter 15
Created to be a Good Steward

*She considers a field and buys it, with the fruit of her hands
she plants a vineyard. Proverbs 31:16 ESV*

*She makes linen garments and sells them; she delivers sashes
to the merchants. Proverbs 31:24 ESV*

The Proverbs 31 woman was prudent with her finances. She made well thought out choices about the items she spent her money on. She identified her specific talents and used those talents to bring extra income to her family. She made shrewd investments with her family's money. She worked hard, remained a good financial steward and she was rewarded.

God desires for all women to be wise with money. He calls us to budget well and not be frivolous with our spending. He tells us not to put our hope in our money and possessions, but rather to keep our eyes focused on Him. He advises us to seek out ways we can bring in extra money so we can bless others. The Lord will always reward those who work hard and manage their funds in a way that honors Him.

*A slack hand causes poverty, but the hand of the diligent
makes rich. Proverbs 10:4 ESV*

A diligent woman is thoughtful with money. She carefully plans out her budget and adheres to it. She rightly assesses desires versus needs and keeps her priorities in order when deciding how to spend her money. She is not excessive and doesn't accrue unnecessary debt. She manages her money well by following wise tips from money experts. Now, I am not exactly the queen of thriftiness, (financial responsibility is definitely an area I struggle in) but I have come a long way and have some tips to share

Here are a few of my favorite ways to save money: 1. Take advantage of sales. This one seems like a no-brainer but something we can often forget to do. Paying attention to sales at the grocery store and stocking up on frequently used items can save a lot of money in the long run. 2. Use credit cards with cash-back options. This is a great way to earn extra money on things you will be purchasing anyway. The key to this is making sure the balance is paid off every month. If you know you don't possess the self-discipline to pay the balance off every month, skip this tip! Pay cash for everything instead. 3. Familiarize yourself with interest rates. Know your options when it comes to eliminating debt and transfer balances to low or no interest cards while you formulate a plan for paying it off. Pay higher interest cards off. Dave Ramsey has a great method for this. If you are able to attend Financial Peace University, I highly recommend it for gaining control of your finances.

As we work diligently and apply wise financial principles to our lives, we will always be rewarded. We reap what we sow. When we are intentional and hard-working it will pay off. There are some who believe God wants His people to live in poverty. They believe money in and of itself is evil. This couldn't be further from the truth for God created everything for us to enjoy.

Without money, who would fund God's kingdom work? Money is a good gift from Him; it just needs to be put in its proper place. We should not chase after money or idolize it in any way. *Love* of money is the true root of all evil and it leads to destruction. We should always be sure to honor God in the area of our finances, just as we do in other aspects of life. Our integrity must remain intact at all times when it comes to money. Because our hearts belong to Jesus money should never be attained by dishonest means, nor should we cheat or lie to save a few dollars.

The getting of treasures by a lying tongue is a fleeting vapor and a snare of death. Proverbs 21:6 ESV

With God there are no "little white lies." When we are deceitful, especially to benefit ourselves, we are not honoring Him. This can range from something big like cheating on our taxes, to something seemingly small like lying about our child's age to get a discount. When we have the right view of God as Holy, we will be careful to honor Him with all of our decisions. When we have the proper view of God as Provider, we will have confidence that He will richly supply every need. We don't need to lie, cheat, or steal to get ahead. We only need to live as He directs, and He will abundantly provide.

For the Lord God is a sun and a shield; the Lord bestows favor and honor. No good thing does He withhold from those who walk uprightly. Psalm 84:11 ESV

And my God will supply every need of yours according to His riches in glory in Christ Jesus. Philippians 4:19 ESV

As the Lord provides our income, we must remember that everything we have belongs to Him. We should always give back to Him first. We should be eager to share and bless others with what we have been given. He doesn't provide us with abundance so that we can become stingy hoarders. He blesses us so we can bless others.

We were created to live in constant gratitude to the Lord for His provision, and to honor Him by giving back to His church and sowing into His kingdom. When we recognize that every monetary blessing comes from Him, the natural response is generosity. When we give to God and to others, He blesses us even more. God promises to take care of us when we take care of His people.

"Give and it will be given to you. Good measure, pressed down, shaken together, running over, will be put into your lap. For with the measure you use it will be measured back to you." Luke 6:38 ESV

Bring the full tithe into the storehouse, that there may be food in my house. And thereby put me to the test, says the Lord of hosts, if I will not open the windows of heaven for you and pour down for you a blessing until there is no more need. Malachi 3:10 ESV

Scripture contains incredible promises for the generous believers who honor God with their finances. I've personally experienced His faithfulness in this many times. God always rewards our obedience in this area. However, we should be careful not to give merely to get. We give because we love God and we want to be obedient to Him. We want to bless His people and see His kingdom advance. We don't give to receive back or because we feel guilty or forced.

The point is this: whoever sows sparingly will also reap sparingly, and whoever sows bountifully will also reap bountifully. Each one must give as he has decided in his heart, not reluctantly or under compulsion, for God loves a cheerful giver. And God is able to make all grace abound to you, so that having all sufficiency in all things at all times, you may abound in every good work. 2 Corinthians 9:6-8 ESV

God designed us to be women who would not elevate money to an idol status in our lives. An idol is anything that takes God's rightful place, anything treasured more than Him. It's what we look to for comfort, assurance, and joy. An idol is what we desire most. God wants to be number one in our lives and in our hearts.

So often the pursuit of wealth is the all consuming force that drives people, rather than a love for Christ. We think money and possessions will bring the contentment and satisfaction we seek after. We let these idols occupy a space in our hearts that should only belong to the Lord. We forget that, in the scope of eternity, this life is very short. A life consumed with the pursuit of wealth is a wasted life. We can take nothing with us into eternity except good deeds done for the kingdom. When we keep an eternity-based mindset, money will not be exalted to an idol status in our lives. We will focus on spending our money in a way that honors God and benefits others, thereby storing up rewards in eternity.

"Do not lay up for yourselves treasures on earth, where moth and rust destroy and where thieves break in and steal, but lay up for yourselves treasures in heaven, where neither moth nor rust destroys and where thieves do not break in and steal. For where your treasure is, there your heart will be also."
Matthew 6:19-21 ESV

Jesus told a story of a rich young man who approached Him seeking answers on how to obtain eternal life. This man kept all the rules and honored God with His outward actions. Yet, God didn't reign in his heart. When Jesus told him to sell all of his possessions to give to the poor and then follow after Him, the man left sorrowful. He wasn't willing to relinquish his hold on his many possessions and allow Jesus first place in his heart. His possessions were an idol that kept him from whole-heartedly following the Lord. Money mattered more to this man than the pursuit of God. His priorities were out of order and it cost him his eternity, just as in the parable of this rich, selfish man:

And he told them a parable, saying, "The land of a rich man produced plentifully, and he thought to himself, 'What shall I do for I have nowhere to store my crops?' And he said, 'I will do this; I will tear down my barns and build larger ones, and there I will store all my grain and my goods. And I will say to my soul, "Soul, you have ample goods laid up for many years; relax, eat, drink, be merry."' But God said to him, 'Fool! This night your soul is required of you, and the things you have prepared, whose will they be?' So is the one who lays up treasure for himself and is not rich toward God.
Luke 12:16-21 ESV

This man was so greedy and selfish that his only concern was acquiring more. He even built new barns to store all of his abundance! He was not rich towards God or others. Money sucked the man in and became the demise of his soul. The Lord knows how easily money and possessions can destroy us. He is well aware of the enemy's scheme to use money to distract us and tempt us into sin.

Satan will dangle materialism in front of us until we are controlled by our want for more. Soon we will find ourselves chasing wealth rather than chasing Jesus. We will never have enough. We think, "If I just made a little more money I'd be happy. If I just had this new car, or that beautiful home." Truth is, it will never be enough. We will never be content with the amount we have. The Bible gives us the recipe for contentment, and it doesn't rest in the size of our bank accounts.

But godliness with contentment is great gain, for we brought nothing into the world, and we cannot take anything out of the world. But if we have food and clothing, with these we will be content. But those who desire to be rich fall into temptation, into a snare, into many senseless and harmful desires that plunge people into ruin and destruction. For the love of money is the root of all kinds of evils.
1 Timothy 6:6-10a ESV

God designed us to be women who would keep money in its rightful place. May we always work hard and use wisdom with our finances. When the Lord provides, let us remember to give thanks for everything He has given us to enjoy. Then, in turn, may we seek to live a life of gratitude and generosity towards God and others. May we forever remember where our hope lies, and never forget that if we have Jesus in our hearts we are rich beyond measure!

Personal Reflection:
Would I consider myself a wise financial steward? Do I budget, plan, and follow smart money principles? Do I spend money frivolously and accrue unnecessary debt?

What steps can I take to gain control of my finances?

What talents do I have that I can use to generate extra income for my family? (Some suggestions: selling baked goods, sewing, child-care, pet-sitting, direct sales, etsy shops.)

What value do I place on money? Does the pursuit of money and "stuff" occupy a place in my heart that should belong only to God? Am I generous with my money and possessions? Do I give to God and to others? Am I content with what I have been given by Him?

Heavenly Father, we thank You for providing everything good for us to enjoy. We know that every gift comes from You and we seek to live lives of gratitude and generosity. We ask Your help in identifying the areas of our lives where we have not been wise financial stewards. Help us to be better planners, better budgeters, and better spenders. Help us to make smart choices with our finances and to keep money in perspective. Reveal to us new ways of providing income so that we can give more to Your kingdom. Reveal to us specific areas of your Kingdom that you would like us to sow into financially. Keep us free from the love of money and the pursuit of materialism. May we hold all You have given us loosely in our hands, because, as Your Word says, life does not consist in the abundance of things we possess. We ask Your forgiveness for anytime money or belongings have taken Your place in our hearts. Realign our priorities and perspectives to be in harmony with Your perfect will. Thank You for all that You do, and all that You are. In Jesus Holy name, Amen.

Chapter 16
Created to be Strong

She dresses herself with strength and makes her arms strong.
Proverbs 31:17 ESV

Strength and dignity are her clothing...
Proverbs 31:25a ESV

Our Creator has designed us to be women of great strength: mind, body, and soul. It is important to remember that, as believers, our bodies are temples of the Holy Spirit and we are responsible for their care. This involves making healthy choices concerning our physical well-being. We can do this by researching the ingredients in the food we consume, the medicines we take, even the products we put onto our skin. Much of our food supply in this day and age is toxic. The best way we can care for our bodies and keep them strong is by being aware of what we allow into them. Our choices set the stage internally for disease to either be encouraged or prevented.

When we take the time to read labels, research ingredients, and investigate where our food comes from, we can honor God by making healthy, informed, choices. Buying food from ethical sources, choosing organic ingredients when possible, and using natural remedies to boost the immune system and to treat many illnesses will go a long way towards keeping our bodies physically strong. Giving our bodies the vitamins and minerals they need and avoiding toxins internally and environmentally keeps our immune system working the way it was designed to. Our Creator has given us everything we need to survive and thrive.

When choosing produce, always go for organic when dealing with dirty dozen fruits and vegetables, as these are the most highly sprayed with pesticides. When purchasing meat or dairy products, avoid growth hormones and meat treated with antibiotics. Choose ethical farms where the farmers treat the animals with kindness, feed them the way God intended them to be fed, and put them out to pasture with plenty of fresh air and sunshine. Avoid cheap, factory-farmed meat. Cheaper is never better when it comes to food quality.

Eat as close to nature as possible by choosing fresh, whole foods rather than packaged and processed goods. When buying anything packaged, stay away from artificial flavors, colors, and preservatives. Select hygiene products that are plant-based rather than artificially scented. These products should always be phthalate and paraben free as well. Everything put on the skin gets absorbed into the skin. Choose products that are as close to nature as possible. If you would like more information on the specifics of removing toxins from your lifestyle, I have a comprehensive, printable guide on exactly what to consume and what to avoid for optimal health available on my website. (You can find my contact information in the back of this book.)

When we avoid toxins we keep our bodies pure. When we eat as God intended we provide our bodies with the minerals and nutrients they need to thrive. As we utilize the plants and herbs He has given us as for natural medicines we will keep our insides strong, and this will be evident on the outside as well. When our bodies are strong, God is honored.

Do you not know that your bodies are temples of the Holy Spirit, who is in you, whom you have received from God? You are not your own; you were bought at a price. Therefore, honor God with your bodies. 1 Corinthians 6:19-20 ESV

A healthy exercise routine and an active life will also keep us strong. The Proverbs 31 woman keeps her arms strong by staying busy. She is constantly working hard and caring for those around her. She is busy around the house, and I don't imagine she wastes too much time lounging around being unproductive. Have you ever noticed that the lazier you are the more you don't want to do anything? I know I have. Motivation gets lost and fatigue takes over. Yet when we keep busy, going from one task to another, we are energized to do more. A body in motion stays in motion. When we stay active we stay strong. A physically strong woman glorifies God with her body.

Therefore, I urge you brothers and sisters, in view of God's mercy, to offer your bodies as a living sacrifice, holy and pleasing to God; this is your true and proper worship.
Romans 12:1 ESV

Along with being created for physical strength, we have also been designed to be strong in soul and spirit. This kind of strength differs in its source. Physical strength is something we cultivate ourselves by living lives of intentionality and discipline. Mental and spiritual strength comes from God. We need to deliberately seek His strength every day. We should dress ourselves with His strength, similar to how we would put on articles of clothing.

Some Bible translations use the phrase "girds herself in strength". The word gird means to surround, enclose, and encircle. I just love the picture this paints. We are to surround ourselves with God's strength. We should enclose ourselves within it. I imagine God's strength as a thick layer of bubble wrap encircled around us that protects us from harm and infuses us with courage and confidence.

He gives power to the faint, and to him who has no might He increases strength. Even youths shall faint and be weary, and young men shall fall exhausted. But they who wait for the Lord shall renew their strength; they shall mount up with wings like eagles; they shall run and not be weary; they shall walk and not faint. Isaiah 40:29-31 ESV

In God's always perfect timing, the week I wrote this chapter coincided with a week I really needed His strength. It seemed like one disappointment after another as I watched the enemy try to destroy the lives of the ones I loved. I felt as if I was suffocating under the weight of my burdens. I was sad, discouraged, and my heart hurt for the pain that was being caused. I could not handle all of this in my own strength. Trying was leaving me weary. Through it all, I knew God was waiting for me to exchange my worries for His strength. He promises His strength will be sufficient for any battle we face.

I had to stop trying to be so strong in my own power, and instead look to Jesus. There's a popular saying that God only gives you what you can handle. It is a well-intentioned consolation, yet it is untrue. The truth is; God helps us handle what we are given. We are not the strong ones. *He* is. It's in the moments of our deepest despair and our most difficult struggles that we realize how much we can lean on Him. He is so dependable.

God is our refuge and strength, a very present help in trouble. Therefore we will not fear though the earth gives way, though the mountains be moved into the heart of the sea, though its waters roar and foam, though the mountains tremble at its swelling. Psalm 46:1-3 ESV

When we go through troubles, we need to implement a strategy that will set the stage for God to fight our battles. The first step is admitting our need for God's help. He already knows what we need, but when we confess our need to Him we are humbled and brought into a position where we can receive His help. Then we get still before the Lord and allow Him to infuse us with His strength. It is during this time of stillness that we are refreshed, strengthened, and given specific direction by the Holy Spirit on what to pray.

Prayer is truly where the battle is won. Never underestimate the power of prayer. Prayer should be our first line of defense against any attack, and our immediate go-to in the face of any adversity. (As I once heard, prayer should be our steering wheel, not our spare tire!) Staying connected to the Father gives us a supernatural strength we could never muster up on our own. Constant prayer keeps us strong. As we pray, we memorize, meditate on, and put our full trust in His promises. And then we live in gratitude, expecting that God will fulfill His Word and provide the strength we need. Here are some of the promises I chose to speak over my life and trust in:

I can do all things through Christ who strengthens me.
Philippians 4:13 ESV

And we know that for those who love God all things work together for good, for those who are called according to His purpose. Romans 8:28 ESV

And I will lead the blind in a way that they do not know, in paths that they have not known I will guide them. I will turn the darkness before them into light, the rough places into level ground. These are the things I do, and I do not forsake them.
Isaiah 42:16 ESV

The first promise reminded me that, through Jesus, I possessed unlimited strength to face any obstacle. The second promise was a mental note that no matter how dire the circumstances seemed; God was working behind the scenes to bring good. And the third promise was the one I could speak over the lives of my troubled loved ones. No matter how dark the situation, no matter how rough and rocky the road, God would make their ways level and illuminate their paths.

Mediating on and praying these promises would remind me that God is in control. It would give me strength for whatever might lie ahead. Spiritual strength for the battles we face will always be found in our Heavenly Father.

The Lord is my strength and my shield; in Him my heart trusts, and I am helped; my heart exults, and with my song I give thanks to Him. The Lord is the strength of His people; He is the saving refuge of his anointed. Psalm 28:7-8 ESV

One of the best Scriptural depictions of unwavering faith in God's strength is found in the story of David and Goliath. David would go on to be a mighty king, but at the time of this story he was just a humble young man who tended to his father's sheep and played music for the king. He was not a warrior, yet he had watched God show up in his life in a powerful way in the past and He knew his God would do it again. He faced a formidable opponent: Goliath was 9 feet tall and covered in bronze armor which weighed 125 pounds in and of itself. He carried a giant spear and was feared by everyone in the nation. No-one dared to step up to his challenge, yet David knew where his strength was found.

And David said, "The Lord who delivered me from the paw of the lion and from the paw of the bear will deliver me from the hand of this Philistine." 1 Samuel 17:37a ESV

David was so reliant upon God's strength that when King Saul tried to lend him his armor for protection, David refused. Instead, he took only his staff, 5 smooth stones, and a sling.

What unwavering confidence and courage that God would fight his battles! He knew God would undoubtedly supply him with whatever he needed to face this giant. And He did!

> *Then David said to the Philistine, "You come to me with a sword and with a spear and with a javelin, but I come to you in the name of the Lord of Hosts, the God of the armies of Israel, whom you have defiled."... When the Philistine arose and came and drew near to meet David, David ran quickly toward the battle line to meet the Philistine. And David put his hand in his bag and took out a stone and slung it and struck the Philistine on his forehead. The stone sank into his forehead, and he fell on his face to the ground.*
> *1 Samuel 17:45, 48-49 ESV*

David's confidence paid off and the giant was defeated. David could never have won this battle on his own. God proved His faithfulness once again. He gave David the strength to be courageous, confident, and victorious in battle. Just as He promises to provide the strength for every single battle we face. We were designed to depend on God in this way. May we be intentional every day to surround ourselves with His strength, and then live with a courageous confidence in His provision. May we stay healthy and strong and live the lives we were created to live: mind, body, and soul.

Personal Reflection:
Do I care for my body and treat it as God's temple? Am I health conscious and aware of the ingredients I consume and their effects on my body? Do I live a fit and active lifestyle? What changes can I make in this area to achieve physical strength and better honor God with my body?

Do I intentionally enclose myself with the strength of the Lord? Do I attempt life in my own power or do I rely on God's strength to see me through?

Is there a particular battle I am facing that I need to release to God? Have I admitted my need to Him and asked for His help? What specific promises can I speak over my life while I wait for God to act? How can I live my 'life in gratitude to show my appreciation for God's provision?

Heavenly Father, we thank You so much for being the supplier of everything we need. We don't have to face a single battle alone, for Your Word says you go before us. You give us strength and power. Because we have You on our side, we know that no giant is too big. You hold an unending, unlimited supply of confidence and courage just waiting to be infused into our spirits. We pray for every situation represented with every one of us who speaks this prayer. We ask You to show Yourself strong as our refuge and help. Help us to rest in the knowledge that You are in control and You are working all things for our good. Give us the faith and confidence of Your servant David, who knew without a doubt His God would come through. Help us to surround ourselves daily with You. To dress ourselves in Your strength. Give us the wisdom and discipline to be physically strong and to make healthy choices that honor You. Show us where and how we can better care for our bodies so we can bring glory to Your name. Thank You for creating us to be strong. Thank You for giving us everything we need to accomplish Your will. In Jesus mighty name, Amen.

Chapter 17
Created to be Compassionate

She opens her hand to the poor and reaches out her hands to the needy. Proverbs 31:20 ESV

From the beginning of Scripture to the end, we see God's consistent concern for the poor and the oppressed. We were created to imitate His compassionate heart, and dedicate our lives to helping the less fortunate. There are so many needy people not only around the world, but in our own cities as well. Worldwide, some are so hungry they eat dirt simply to fill their bellies. Others sell their children into slavery just for a chance at a better life. In our own communities there are needy people everywhere we turn. We have a foster care system jam packed with children who are desperate for loving families. Our prisons are overflowing with hopeless and hurting adults. Poverty is everywhere. Here are some alarming statistics:

*Nearly half the world lives on less than $2.50 a day
*22,000 children die a day due to poverty
*More than 750 million people lack adequate access to clean drinking water
*Hunger is the number one cause of death worldwide

It's easy to forget statistics like this exist when we live in the comfort and luxury of first world countries. Even those who think themselves poor by culture's standards are far richer than they realize when compared with much of the world. We need to open our eyes to the many disadvantaged around us. Christians especially should be the frontrunners in fostering and adoption, as well as in providing food and care for the needy. An often asked question is why there are so many needy people if we have a good God? The truth is, if we lived as He directed and shared His concern for the poor, this would be a different world. We are Jesus' representatives on earth and are expected to be His hands and feet and care for the broken and hurting. It is our God given responsibility.

"Is not this the kind of fasting I have chosen: to loose the chains of injustice and untie the cords of the yoke, to set the oppressed free and break every yoke? Is it not to share your food with the hungry and to provide the poor wanderer with shelter –when you see the naked, to clothe them, and not to turn away from your own flesh and blood?" Isaiah 58:6-7 NIV

God's intention has always been for His followers to provide for the needy. This goes all the way back to the Old Testament, when God instituted multiple laws to be sure the Israelites would notice and care for the needy among them, rather than ignore or take advantage of those who were poor. God's merciful heart for the poor and oppressed is weaved all throughout the Old and New Testaments. In the New Testament we see Jesus, who is the image of the invisible God, constantly extending Himself for the needy. Healing the sick. Giving sight to the blind. Cleansing lepers and setting the oppressed free. This was His God-given mission as well.

"The Spirit of the Lord is upon me, because he has anointed me to proclaim good news to the poor. He has sent me to proclaim liberty to the captives and recovering of sight to the blind, to set at liberty those who are oppressed."
Luke 4:18 ESV

We can follow in Jesus' footsteps by identifying and meeting the needs of those who desperately need help. Let's discuss some practical ways we can spend our time, talents, and treasures helping those who are less fortunate than us. The first way we can help is with our time.

First, we must simply take the time to notice, really notice, that there are broken people everywhere. It's easy to be so caught up in our own lives and the whirlwind of busy days that we don't see the needs around us crying out for help. The homeless person on the corner who could really use a hot meal and a conversation. The orphan who waits day after day for a family. The prisoner who desperately needs the love and hope of Jesus.

Jesus went out of His way to minister to hurting people. He met physical needs as He healed the sick and fed the hungry. He also met the spiritual needs of many by lovingly confronting their sin and revealing Himself as the source of abundant and eternal life.

In the story of the woman at the well, we see Jesus going out of His way to address the spiritual need of a Samaritan woman who had been outcast and shunned by society. This woman was living with man number six, after having already been through five husbands. In a culture where Jewish people and Samaritans didn't get along, just the fact that Jesus sat talking with this woman would have been considered scandalous by many.

Yet, Jesus knew that underneath this woman's sinful behavior lie a deeper spiritual need which could only be met by Him. This woman may have been looked down upon by others, but not Jesus. Her soul mattered to Jesus. He made sure to be at that well at exactly the right time. He revealed Himself to her, spoke truth, and became a catalyst for change in this needy woman's life.

When we take the time to identify and then meet the physical and spiritual needs of others, we walk the same path

Jesus walked. When we put aside our own agenda and spend time with people who God considers valuable and precious, He is honored. We are also instructed to speak up for those who cannot speak for themselves. There are many important causes to which we can lend our voice and our time. This world needs more compassionate and passionate people, and we were created to be the women to fill that void.

Learn to do good; seek justice, correct oppression; bring justice to the fatherless, plead the widow's cause. Isaiah 1:17 ESV

On the flip side of being blind to the needs around us, we can also feel completely overwhelmed because there are *so many* needs. It can be hard to distinguish which needs God is specifically asking us to fill. The answer to this is to discover our talents and the particular calling God has placed in our hearts.

For myself, I have always had a desire to help hurting children. This is a desire God planted in my heart early on, based on my life experiences, and then He used that desire to direct me to the specific group of people He wanted me to focus on. I still keep my eyes open for other ways I can help the needy (as God brings the opportunity), but my primary time, talent, and treasure goes towards helping disadvantaged children.

This part will look different for everyone. Some, like me, will be called to help orphans or children in some way, which may include fostering and/or adoption. Others may have a passion for helping the homeless or disadvantaged women. Still others will be called toward prison ministry. If you are not sure exactly what needs God wants you to fill, ask Him! He will make it clear to you, for His desire for all of us is that we are moved to compassionate action. Action being the key word; our compassion should always move us to action.

But if anyone has the world's goods and sees his brother in need, yet closes his heart against him, how does God's love abide in him? Little children, let us not love in word or talk but in deed and in truth. 1 John 3:17-18 ESV

Having a compassionate heart is a necessity, yet if we do nothing with that compassion, it is wasted. We must act. We must help. We must spend our time, talent, and treasure on what matters most.

I once heard a story of two working men. Each man contemplated what they would purchase when payday came around. The first man thought only of himself. The first paycheck came and he bought himself a big soft reclining chair so he could lounge around in comfort. The next paycheck he received he bought a surround sound speaker system he could install into the chair so he could listen to his sports and television with pristine sound. The following week he bought himself a new television because he planned to spend a lot of time in his comfy chair. And on and on it went; one self-indulgent choice after another.

The second man chose to look outside of himself and see how his treasure could benefit another. His first paycheck was used to buy two rocking chairs, one for himself, and one so he could invite a friend over to spend time together. The second payday that came around he spent his extra money treating that friend to dinner. The following week he noticed his friend's shoes looking pretty worn so he bought him a new pair. This continued on as the man constantly sought out ways to bless others with his money.

When we make the intentional choice to use our resources to help others, God is glorified in so many ways. I love this quote from John Piper, in his book, *Don't waste your life:*

"Using our possessions in a way that makes the most needy glad in God would save us in more ways than one. It would confirm that Christ is our Treasure, and thus keep us on the path to heaven. And it would transform our society, which is driven by the suicidal craving to satisfy itself with no joy in Christ and no love for the needy." (Piper, 2011)

How beautifully said! We must ask ourselves, where is our treasure found? Is it in our belongings and the fleeting pleasures of self-indulgence, or is it found in Jesus? When Jesus is our treasure we will hold on to everything else loosely. We will be generous with our money and possessions.

In this way, society will be transformed one act of mercy at a time. Our lives will have meaning and purpose. When that glorious day comes that we see Jesus face to face, we can say we truly lived for Him, as we became His hands and feet on this Earth.

"Then the king will say to those on his right, 'Come, you who are blessed by my Father, inherit the kingdom prepared for you from the foundation of the world. For I was hungry and you gave me food, I was thirsty and you gave me drink, I was a stranger and you welcomed me, I was naked and you clothed me, I was sick and you visited me, I was in prison and you came to me.' Then the righteous will answer him saying, 'Lord, when did we see you hungry and feed you, or thirsty and give you drink? And when did we see you a stranger and welcome you, or naked and clothe you?' And the King will answer them, 'Truly, I say to you, as you did it to one of the least of these my brothers, you did it to me.'"
Matthew 25:34-40 ESV

Personal Reflection:

Are my eyes opened to the many needs around me? Do I take the time to notice and look for ways that I can help?
What talents or passions do I have that can direct me toward a specific group of people God wants me to help?

What steps do I need to take to connect my compassion with action?

Heavenly Father, we praise You and thank You for Your compassionate heart towards the poor and oppressed. We know You see every tragedy and every injustice. You are there amidst the suffering, and promise one day to wipe away every tear. Until that day comes, we know you created us to be Your hands and feet on this earth. We pray for renewed passion to help the needy. Open our eyes to the hurting people around us. Show us ways we can help. Give us specific direction on where we should focus our time, talents, and treasures. Make our paths cross with those who need our help the most. We pray for a revival in the hearts of Christian men and women everywhere, to live out this calling and bring Your love to others. We pray for Your continued deliverance of the needy. May practical needs all over this world be met: food provided, clean drinking water established, and poverty eradicated. We pray for those who are being oppressed, those who cannot speak up for themselves, that justice would prevail and light would overcome the darkness. Help us to stay focused on this most important mission rather than being consumed by self-indulgence and materialism. Make a way for us to bless others as we have been so abundantly blessed. In Jesus Holy name, Amen.

Chapter 18
Created to be Ready

She is not afraid of snow for her household, for all her household are clothed in scarlet. Proverbs 31:21 ESV

The Proverbs 31 woman prepares beforehand so she will be ready to handle whatever comes her way. We see in this Scripture she is prepared well in advance for every turn of the season. She has readied her household for the snowy winter that lies ahead of them. She is a careful and thoughtful planner, and her attention to detail ensures that her family will have everything they need, when they need it.

This concept of preparation reaffirms what we have already discussed; that we created to be the keepers of our homes. When the home is overseen with diligence, a by-product of that will be a well-prepared household. We were created to be this prudent woman, and use our time wisely in the management of our homes.

We can stay prepared by being efficient with our time and planning accordingly. My favorite tool for staying ahead of the game is my daily planner. (I'm old-school so I need to write everything out.) I love planners with space for every hour of the day to be planned out. I don't always need to be this organized, but sometimes it's necessary! In our planners we can keep track of our appointments, write out our to-do lists, even schedule our time with the Lord.

What has been extra helpful to me, in addition to my planner, is having a weekly dry-erase board on display in my kitchen. Sunday nights I write out my major appointments for the coming week on this board as well as my weekly meal plan. I also add in any errands or things I want to accomplish that week. Planning out my meals over the weekend and writing out my shopping list keeps me prepared and ready to feed my family throughout the week. This eliminates the need for extra spending or unhealthy fast food choices.

While it is our responsibility to anticipate and prepare for the physical needs of our families; the most crucial preparation we can ever make is to be sure we are ready for Jesus to return. The Bible says this day will come like a thief in the night. Although believers differ on interpreting the order of specific end time events, one thing is clear: there will come a day when God's patience runs out, and His judgment on wickedness will be revealed. Every person on this earth will either embrace Jesus as their Lord and Savior, or face Him as their judge.

"When the Son of Man comes in his glory, and all the angels with him, then He will sit on his glorious throne. Before Him will be gathered all the nations, and He will separate people one from another as a shepherd separates the sheep from the goats." Matthew 25:31-32 ESV

As believers, this will be a day to rejoice! Jesus, our good shepherd, will finally return for us, His sheep. He will return for those eagerly anticipating His arrival, to take us to a place where peace reigns forever, and death and sadness are no more. This is the day we look towards and live for. We can stay prepared by daily examining our lives to be sure we are living for eternity. Our lives should show our readiness and anticipation of Jesus' return. We should be actively pursuing a kingdom lifestyle that is marked by faith, good works, holiness, and love. Keeping in mind that Jesus could return at any time keeps us from living irresponsibly.

But the day of the Lord will come like a thief, and then the heavens will pass away with a roar, and the heavenly bodies will be burned up and dissolved, and the earth and the works that are done on it will be exposed. Since all these things are thus to be dissolved, what sort of people ought you to be in lives of holiness and godliness, waiting for and hastening the coming day of God, because of which the heavens will be set on fire and dissolved, and the heavenly bodies will melt as they burn! 2 Peter 3:10-12 ESV

Imagine you have guests coming over for dinner. Not just any guests, but the CEO of your husband's prestigious company and his wife will be visiting your home for the first time. I don't know about you, but I would love to make a good first impression. I would have the meal planned out and shopped for the day before. I would take extra care to make sure the table was set beautifully. I would want my home to look spotless and to have a cozy and inviting feel. The family would be dressed nicely, in anticipation of our guests' arrival. Would you do the same?

If we would take such care in this situation; then how much more should we prepare for the return of Jesus? Christ is said to be returning for a spotless church. To be this type of pure church we must keep our focus on God and not allow ourselves to be distracted by the things of this world. Our aim should be to grow in the grace and knowledge of Jesus.

For this very reason, make every effort to supplement your faith with virtue and virtue with knowledge, and knowledge with self-control, and self-control with steadfastness, and steadfastness with godliness, and godliness with brotherly affection, and brotherly affection with love. For if these qualities are yours and are increasing, they keep you from being ineffective or unfruitful in the knowledge of our Lord Jesus Christ. 2 Peter 1:5-8 ESV

Peter is not advocating for a passive faith in this passage. Rather, he insists we must actively pursue the things of God to be ready for Jesus to return. Peter goes on in this letter to remind believers to practice these qualities so they will be prepared to meet Jesus face to face. He also advises believers to watch out for false prophets and false teachers, which will rise up to deceive many. The best way we can keep from being deceived is to stay grounded in the Bible. We should never put 100% trust in any teacher or preacher; rather we should constantly search the Scriptures to be sure what we are being taught lines up with God's truth.

Beloved, do not believe every spirit, but test the spirits to see whether they are from God, for many false prophets have gone out into the world. 1 John 4:1 ESV

As we grow in our knowledge of the Bible, we should also be steadily growing in our obedience to God's words. Practicing righteousness should become a part of our daily living. We should continually surrender ourselves to God's will. and ask for His grace to empower us to live the lives He created us to live. In this way, we will be prepared for the day when we meet Jesus face to face. Jesus spoke many parables illustrating the need to be ready and waiting for Him.

In one such parable, He tells a story of ten virgins who were waiting for the bridegroom. To better understand this parable let's delve into some history. In Jewish culture, after a man and a woman were betrothed to be married, there was a preparation period during which each person would get ready for the marriage. This period sometimes lasted up to a year. Once the groom finished preparing, it was time to collect his bride-to-be from her home and escort her to a wedding celebration at the groom's house. This was typically done at night. The groom marched with his male companions to the bride's home, torches lighting the way. The bride would be waiting at her home with her female companion. She would be unaware of the exact time when the groom would arrive, but she would remain prepared for that to happen at any moment.

In this parable, only five of the women were ready to join the bridegroom. The other five had no oil for their lamps and became drowsy and fell asleep. When they realized the bridegroom was coming, they begged the wise virgins for some of their oil, yet it was too late. There was not enough to share. In the end, the unprepared ones were left out of the wedding feast. Those who stayed watching and alert left with the bride-groom to attend the joyful celebration. In this same manner, we are called to be awake and prepared at all times for our Lord to return; ready and waiting to celebrate.

"Blessed are those servants whom the master finds awake when he comes. You also must be ready, for the Son of Man is coming at an hour you do not expect." Luke 12:37a, 40 ESV

When our Master returns, will we be ready for Him? Have we prioritized teaching His ways to our children so they can be prepared as well? Half-hearted living and lukewarm faith will not prepare us for eternity. Embracing Jesus as Savior but not submitting to Him as Lord does not put us in the position to be warmly embraced at His coming, rather; the Scriptures say those who know the Father's will yet refuse to submit and obey will be *left out* of God's kingdom. Truly, nothing is more important than making sure we are obedient and ready, and this is done by following Jesus whole-heartedly.

End times signs are all around us as warfare and natural disasters increase. False teachings abound and I think we can all agree; this world is getting more and more evil by the day. Steps towards a one world government and the rise of the Antichrist are well under way. Technological advances necessary for end times Bible prophecies to be fulfilled are already here. Jesus tells us not to obsess about end-time events, for no one knows the day or the hour, but to be aware and ready. Regardless of when that day occurs, any day could be our last and we must be sure we are prepared to meet Jesus face to face.

Keeping with the theme of careful planning, one way we can stay on top of being prepared for this day is by writing down spiritual goals for ourselves and family. Goal setting is important, and no priority is greater than drawing closer to God and living a life that brings honor to His name. We should aim to identify a few things God is working on with us during any given season of our lives. It is helpful to write these things out and set goals for change. We can write out corresponding Scriptures and active steps we can take in order to achieve each goal.

One area God is working on with me currently is my patience level (or lack there-of). So in order to partner with the Holy Spirit to bring about change in this area, I can memorize Scriptures to remind myself that love is patient, and a servant of God must be patient towards everyone. I can look for spiritual books that deal with the subject of patience, kindness, and love. I can seek out classes or groups at my church that help grow these attributes in the life of a Christian. As I do this, I will grow. Then I can re-evaluate my list in a few months to see how I have grown and then prayerfully consider where God wants to grow me next.

Friends, I know we have discussed some hard truths today. My intention is not to make any true believer question their salvation or loyalty to Christ, but rather to implore each of us to examine our lives for evidence of our faith. We must evaluate ourselves to be sure our love for Jesus is resulting in righteous living.

When we take the time to examine our faith, we can be sure we are ready in every way for what is to come. While it is important to prepare daily, and for the future, nothing takes precedence over preparing our family for the day we will meet our Maker. May we set about this preparation with focus, diligence, and joy; and look forward with anticipation to the day we will meet our Maker.

And I heard a loud voice from the throne saying, "Behold, the dwelling place of God is with man. He will dwell with them, and they will be his people, and God himself will be with them as their God. He will wipe away every tear from their eyes, and death shall be no more, neither shall there be mourning, nor crying, nor pain anymore, for the former things have passed away." Revelation 21:3-4 ESV

Personal Reflection:
Am I claiming Jesus as Savior without submitting to Him as Lord? If the answer is yes, confess a heartfelt prayer of repentance to God and ask Him to reveal areas of your life that aren't in alignment with His will.

Am I prepared and ready for the day I will meet Jesus face to face? Am I actively pursuing Him and as a result living a life marked by a progression in holiness and good works? Have I prepared my children for that day as well?

Can I name one to three areas God is currently at work in my life to transform me into the image of Christ? How can I stay focused on my spiritual growth in these areas?

Do I take the time to be sure the physical needs of my family are met? Am I an effective planner and well organized? What steps can I take to be better prepared in general?

Heavenly Father, we praise Your name and we thank You for Your Word to us today. Please open our ears and our hearts to receive Your Truth. Thank You for reminding us to keep our focus on You and on eternity. This life is but a vapor, and we know everything we do here will echo into eternity. Help us to make good, God-honoring choices. Keep us centered on Jesus and living lives marked with love, holiness, and truth. Help us to examine ourselves often to be sure we are on the right track. Keep us from being deceived by false teachers. Bring to mind any areas of our lives that are not being lived in obedience to Your will and show us how to align ourselves with Your truth. Forgive us for the times we have wanted all the blessings of salvation with none of the sacrifice. Thank You for being a loving God, full of mercy and grace for those who call on You from a pure and humble heart. We pray You will continue to empower us daily to live for You. Help us to identify and prepare for the needs of our families. Where organizational skills lack, equip us to be better. Give us wisdom and guide us into Your will. Help us to prepare, plan, and meet every household need, so we can embody all that it means to be a Proverbs 31 woman. In Jesus Precious name, Amen.

Chapter 19

Created to be Courageous

She laughs without fear of the future.
Proverbs 31:25b NLT

Picture this Proverbs 31 woman with me. I imagine her skipping through a field of flowers and sunshine. Long flowing dress, wavy hair bouncing in the wind. Smiling, laughing, care-free. Do you long to be this woman? I know I do! Truth is each and every one of us has been created to be this woman. We were created to know God and experience Him daily in such a way that peace would reign in our hearts.

What if we got this truth deep down into our souls? Fear would be demolished. Courage would abound. We would boldly approach life knowing the very hairs on our head have been numbered by our Father in heaven. We would hold fast to the truth that we belong to Him and our lives are forever held by Him. He is in control, therefore; there is nothing to fear. Ever.

"Therefore I tell you, do not be anxious about your life, what you will eat or what you will drink, nor about your body, what you will put on. Is not life more than food, and the body more than clothing? Look at the birds of the air; they neither sow nor reap nor gather into barns, and yet your heavenly Father feeds them. Are you not of more value than they? And which of you by being anxious can add a single hour to his span of life." Matthew 6:25-27 ESV

These words of Jesus are so beautiful, aren't they? What a powerful reminder that He is always with us. Yet, we forget this truth far too often. We allow fear to consume us, to dictate our decisions, to rob us of the peace God wants to instill into our souls. Fear is one of Satan's favorite weapons. He knows if he can get us to operate out of a place of fear, he has won. He will use our fear to paralyze us in inaction, disturb our peace, limit our victories, and keep us from being obedient to God's will. Yet, when we take a stand and refuse to be ruled by fear, we can step out in faith and do whatever it is God asks of us. He will give us the courage to proceed; we just need to take that first step of faith. When we believe without a doubt that God is in control, fear's hold on us diminishes and peace flourishes. Peace is promised by Jesus to all of His followers.

"I am leaving you with a gift – peace of mind and heart. And the peace I give is a gift the world cannot give. So don't be troubled or afraid." John 14:27 NLT

Jesus makes it clear; the peace He offers cannot be found anywhere else. We cannot obtain this peace from anyone or anything in this world. The things of this world *bring* fear and anxiety. We are living in troubled times, with plenty to worry about. Yet, when we fix our eyes on Jesus, we are reminded of who is in control. He assures us He will never leave us nor forsake us. God pours out on us the gift of peace and the promise of His presence, which in turn puts fear in its place.

"Fear not, for I have redeemed you; I have called you by name, you are mine. When you pass through the waters, I will be with you; and through the rivers, they shall not overwhelm you; when you walk through the fire you shall not be burned and the flame shall not consume you." Isaiah 43:1-2 ESV

It is important to note the word when in these passages. God's call to fearless living is not a guarantee of a trouble-free existence. Trials and suffering are a part of this broken world, and believers are not exempt. Rather, this Scripture reminds us that we can live courageously through our trials because God is always with us. The water shall not *overwhelm* us. The fire shall not *consume* us. God's Word communicates to us that our struggles do not have the final say. The Lord will work all things for our good. He will be present in the midst of every trial, pouring out His promised peace and comfort. What shall we fear when we know nothing can separate us from the Lord?

No, in all these things we are more than conquerors through Him who loved us. For I am sure that neither death nor life, nor angels nor rulers, nor things present nor things to come, nor powers, nor height nor depth, nor anything else in all creation, will be able to separate us from the love of God in Christ Jesus our Lord. Romans 8:37-38 ESV

If that isn't a reason to banish fear and live confidently in the providence of our Heavenly Father, I don't know what is! We can trust in God's protective care. We can rest assured; He is for us and not against us. We can courageously approach every single day, with the knowledge that God is beside us: leading, comforting, and directing our steps. He is our Protector, our Healer, our Deliverer. Our Mighty Counselor, our Savior, our Father. When we trust Him and we seek Him we will be able to say with the psalmist David,

I sought the Lord and He answered me and He delivered me from all my fears. Psalm 34:4 ESV

To live fearlessly, our eyes must remain fixed upon Jesus, not our circumstances. When we focus on what is going on around us rather than the One who is in us, directing our steps, fear sets in and keeps us from victory and breakthrough. Fear can also keep us out of God's will and, as we see with the Israelites, have detrimental consequences. The Israelites had seen numerous displays of God's miraculous powers as He freed them from Egyptian slavery. They watched as He rained plagues upon the evil Pharaoh and then split the Red Sea so they could walk through to safety. He literally fed them from heaven as they journeyed, yet so quickly they forgot who was in control! They were led to the Promised Land, which God promised to help them conquer. Spies were sent out and told to report back their findings about the land and its inhabitants. The report did not seem favorable towards the Israelites.

And they told him, "We came to the land to which you sent us. It flows with milk and honey, and this is its fruit. However, the people who dwell in the land are strong, and the cities are fortified and very large." Numbers 13:27-28a ESV

Circumstances se*emed* bleak. The cities were fortified and inhabited by literal giants called Nephilim, pretty frightening! Looking at this through their natural eyes there seemed to be no way. Yet, God had promised to be with them. I wish I could say the Israelites trusted God whole-heartedly and stepped out in faith but that just isn't the story. Instead, they chose to focus on the seemingly insurmountable challenge of conquering the city. They cowered in fear. They complained and cried out against the supposed unfairness of God for leading them to the land where they were sure they would meet their demise. They even began to conceive a plan to go back to Egypt, to slavery!

Only two men, Caleb and Joshua, were confident. They knew with God on their side they had nothing to fear. They tried to convince the others but to no avail.

"If the Lord delights in us, He will bring us into this land and give it to us, a land that flows with milk and honey. Only do not rebel against the Lord. And do not fear the people of the land, for they are bread for us. Their protection is removed from them, and the Lord is with us; do not fear them."
Numbers 14:8-9 ESV

Yet still, the Israelites refused to listen. They allowed their fear of what was seen overrule trust in their unseen God. They lacked the courage to follow through on God's plan and step out in faith. Ultimately, this fear cost an entire generation of Israelites the blessing of the Promised Land. Because of their complaining, whining, and downright refusal to trust God and move forward, they were sent back into the wilderness for forty years.

So how can we avoid getting stuck in our own wilderness experiences? By trusting God and moving forward in faith when He says move. By keeping our eyes on the very One who orchestrates our lives, not on the shifting circumstances *of* our lives.

"Have I not commanded you? Be strong and courageous. Do not be frightened, and do not be dismayed, for the Lord your God is with you wherever you go." Joshua 1:9 ESV

Much of my life was spent in the soul-crushing grip of fear. This stemmed from my extremely unstable and chaotic childhood. At a young age, I turned to drugs and alcohol to ease my anxiety and quiet my fears. When I was intoxicated I didn't have a care in the world. Yet, in the moments of sobriety between my party weekends, fear, anxiety, and obsessive thoughts would rear their ugly heads. I tried to solve the problem by popping prescription pills, doing whatever I could to achieve peace of mind.

Yet, medicine is just a surface-level answer. It only masks the symptoms, never actually addressing the root of the problem. I didn't want to be addicted to prescription drugs yet I didn't want to live my life in fear. I was tired of the constant what-if's and an imagination that ran wild with worst case scenarios. Fear of sickness and death for myself and loved ones.

When my relationship with the Lord deepened and I stopped abusing drugs and alcohol, the new channel for my anxiety became an unhealthy obsession with my family's health. I became convinced that if we were exposed to any toxins, in any way, a cancer diagnosis would be just around the corner. I'm sure I drove my husband (and many others) at least a little crazy.

Four years ago, when my youngest son was born, I hit the ultimate high of my health obsession. My natural instinct to protect and nurture my child coupled with too much information readily accessible on the internet became a catalyst for my anxieties to form into a full blown obsession. Obsession with everything my child came in contact with. Obsession over every single thing he ate. An irrational conviction that unless he was with me, under my (self-proclaimed) unmatchable care, something horrible would happen.

Then one day, God shattered my little bubble of self-reliance. Literally. My boys love to play hide and seek and one of their favorite and most predictable, hiding spots is our guest room closet. This closet is basically the storage for everything that doesn't have a place in the house so it is quite full and slightly disorganized. Boxes and blankets are stacked on top of each other; shelves are full of everything from shoeboxes of old photos to random costume accessories.

On this particular day, I went to search for something in the closet, and stumbled upon a life-changing moment. On the floor was an 8x10 glass picture frame, shattered in a hundred pieces. As I picked it up off the floor, my heart raced. The kids had been playing in there just that very morning. How close had they come to hurting themselves? Visions of ambulance rides and hospital trips danced through my head.

It was in that moment God spoke the profound words which ushered His true peace into my life. "It's not you keeping them safe," the Holy Spirit whispered into my heart. "It's me." This truth sank deep into my soul and has settled there ever since. Though I have a God-given responsibility to care for mine and my families bodies and make good choices when it comes to our health; ultimately our fate is in His hands, not mine.

There is a fine line between awareness and implementation of healthy practices and all out obsession with health. I had crossed that line long ago. I lived, even as a Bible-believing, Christ-follower, bound by fear and enslaved by anxiety. I lived under the delusion that if I could control every little thing, nothing bad would ever happen to me or to my family.

The enemy used my past, and a weakness I had never dealt with, to build a stronghold in my mind and prevent me from walking in the peace and victory Christ died for me to have. The control I thought I had over my circumstances perpetuated the illusion that I had nothing to fear. Yet, I was far from true peace. Fear and control were two sides of the same coin, and it all led back to the fact that I did not take hold of the peace of Jesus for myself, nor did I live like I truly believed God was in control.

"Are not two sparrows sold for a penny? And not one of them will fall to the ground apart from your Father. But even the hairs of your head are all numbered. Fear not, therefore; you are of more value than many sparrows."
Matthew 10:29-31 ESV

Fear releases its paralyzing grip on our lives when we truly believe God is in control. Our Heavenly Father knows how frequently His children can become anxious about the future, and how quickly the enemy of our souls will use this fear to cripple us. That's why we find over eighty Scriptures in which God tells His people not to fear. When we meditate on these Scriptures and remind ourselves of them often, anxieties about the future will melt away. When we consistently replace each worrisome thought that enters our minds with God's truth, we will begin to break free from fear.

Now that I have a proper understanding of God's providence, I can live peacefully. I still eat clean and am passionate about healthy living, yet it is no longer an all out obsession. I do the best I can to honor God with my body and trust Him for the rest. I know it isn't the amount of supplements I take or organic vegetables I eat that determines my destiny, it is God alone. He has already pre-determined the length of my life, and He has written every one of my days in His book.

Your eyes saw my unformed body; all the days ordained for me were written in your book before one of them came to be.
Psalm 139:16 ESV

Not one thing will happen to us that God does not have the power to redeem, restore, and ultimately bring good out of. And He promises to be with us every step of the way. We are His precious children, valuable to Him and dearly loved. Imagine your love for your own children, your fierce desire to nurture, cherish, and protect them. Then multiply that times about a million. God is infinitely better at nurturing, cherishing, and protecting His children than we could ever be.

When we rest in that knowledge and live like we really believe it is true, tranquility will reign in our hearts. When tranquility reigns in our hearts, courage will abound in our actions. We don't have to fear the future because we know God is in control, and He is with us. When we seek Him out and cast our cares on Him, we make an amazing exchange: our worries for His promised peace. I'll take that trade any day!

Do not be anxious about anything, but in every situation, by prayer and petition, with thanksgiving, present your requests to God. And the peace of God, which transcends all understanding, will guard your hearts and your minds in Christ Jesus. Philippians 4:6-7 ESV

Personal Reflection:
Do I tend to worry about the future? Am I fearful of all the what-if's in life? If the answer is yes, what specific promises of God can I memorize and focus on to alleviate my fears?

During the storms of life, are my eyes fixed on Jesus, confident He is in control? Do I allow myself to feel defeated or discouraged due to my circumstances or do I have faith in God's guidance and assurance He will bring me through every trial?

Has there been something specific God has asked me to do that I've been putting off because I am fearful of the outcome? What steps can I take to purposefully and obediently move forward in faith?

Heavenly Father, we are so grateful for Your precious Word today. Thank You for the truth that sets us free. Thank You for Your provision and protection, Your comfort and Your guidance. We know with You on our side, we have absolutely nothing to fear. You hold our lives in Your infinitely competent hands. Whatever this world may throw our way, Your promise of peace will always be with us. Help us daily to cast all of our anxieties and cares on You. Help us to live obediently and courageously, stepping forward in faith whenever You call us to move. Fix our gaze above, on Jesus, never on our circumstances. We know You are in control and the hairs on our very heads are numbered. As believers in Jesus, we belong to You. Thank You for loving us like You do. We pray for those who struggle with anxiety and fearful thoughts. We pray You would set them free and break the strongholds the enemy has erected in their minds. Abolish fear and replace it with peace, the peace only Jesus can bring. Fill us all with Your Holy Spirit and empower us by Your grace to live courageously, for Your glory. In Jesus name, Amen.

Chapter 20
Created to be Wise

She opens her mouth with wisdom...
Proverbs 31:26a ESV

God created us to be women of intelligence, skill, and sound judgment. We are called to speak words of wisdom and make wise choices. As we diligently seek after knowledge and understanding we will store up wisdom within ourselves that can be drawn from when needed. In order to acquire wisdom, it is important we know where it comes from. Wisdom does not come from within:

Do you see a man who is wise in his own eyes? There is more hope for a fool than for him. Proverbs 26:12 ESV

It does not come from culture:

For the wisdom of this world is foolishness in God's sight. As it is written; "He catches the wise in their craftiness".
1 Corinthians 3:19 NIV

So if we can't find wisdom inside of us, or around us; where *can* we find it?

From where does wisdom come? And where is the place of understanding? It is hidden from the eyes of all living and concealed from the birds of the air. God understands the way to it, and He knows its place. For He looks to the ends of the earth and sees everything under the heavens.
Job 28:20-21,23-24 ESV

True wisdom is found in God and God alone. He is the Maker of all things. He stretched out the heavens and put every star in its place. Light burst forth at His command. He spoke; the mountains were formed and the oceans were set into place. He intricately and uniquely designed every creature on this planet, including us. He knows all, sees all, and is the source of all wisdom. There is no-one better to seek wisdom from than the One who created our very lives with His breath. God is the source of infinite knowledge. As we seek His wisdom, He will guide us and direct our steps.

Trust in the Lord with all your heart, and do not lean on your own understanding. In all your ways acknowledge Him, and He will make straight your paths. Be not wise in your own eyes. Proverbs 2:5-7a ESV

God promises to make our paths straight when we look to Him for wisdom in our daily lives. I don't know about you, but I would much rather trust the Creator of the universe to lead me than to rely on my own limited perspective and fickle feelings for guidance! I like to congratulate myself on my own intelligence from time to time but as clever as I *think* I might be; I didn't create the astonishing wonder of life. Nor did I draw out the blueprint for this solar system and devise a plan from the beginning of time to redeem every fallen creature on this earth. Yes, God's wisdom is infinitely beyond anything I could ever think or understand. Even still, He invites us all to partake of His wisdom simply by asking.

If any of you lacks wisdom, you should ask God, who gives generously to all without finding fault, and it will be given to you. James 1:5 NIV

God is such a good Father! He promises to provide wisdom and guidance whenever we ask. He didn't create us to then abandon us to fumble around in life with no direction or guidance. He longs for us to look to Him and depend on Him to lead us. The best way to cultivate wisdom is by reading God's Word. The Bible is bursting with priceless treasures just waiting to be discovered by us. Everything we will need to navigate life is found within its pages. Timeless wisdom. Infinite knowledge. We read the Bible and we learn how to relate to God, and how we should relate to others. We learn about the boundaries God has put into place to protect us. We find out how we can live a life that honors God and brings peace to our souls.

But the wisdom from above is first pure, then peaceable, gentle, open to reason, full of mercy and good fruits, impartial and sincere. James 3:17 ESV

All Scripture is God-breathed and is useful for teaching, rebuking, correcting and training in righteousness, so that the servant of God may be thoroughly equipped for every good work. 2 Timothy 3:16-17 NIV

As I've mentored women who are new in the faith, the obstacle I've heard repeatedly is that the Bible seems intimidating and hard to understand. Those who have never read it before are discouraged to even try because they feel as if they must be some sort of spiritual giant to understand its words. If this is your struggle please know this is a lie from the enemy meant to keep you from God's Word. God wrote the

Bible for us, for *you*! He wants you to understand it. Don't let fear or discouragement keep you from His Word.

Choose an easy to read translation (I especially love study Bibles with built-in commentary) and pray beforehand for God's guidance. He will illuminate the words as you read, and teach you exactly what He wants you to learn every time you open those beautiful pages. You will soon find that not only are you reading the Bible, but the Bible is actually reading you.

I always pray for God's wisdom before I read, for it is His Holy Spirit that opens eyes and imparts understanding. He teaches me something new every time, and provides me with priceless wisdom for specific situations that I am facing. His Word is an unending supply of life-giving guidance and I couldn't imagine life without it.

For the Lord gives wisdom; from His mouth come knowledge and understanding; He stores up sound wisdom for the upright; He is a shield to those who walk in integrity, guarding the paths of justice and watching over the way of his saints. Then you will understand righteousness and justice and equity, every good path; for wisdom will come into your heart, and knowledge will be pleasant to your soul.
Proverbs 2:6-10 ESV

We must make sure that, as we read the Bible and seek God's wisdom, His words will fall on a softened heart that desires to be obedient to Him. It is not enough to simply read about God's will, we must be ready to *do* God's will. Wisdom is of no avail if we are unwilling to heed God's advice and live as He directs.

Jesus tells a parable of a man who goes out to sow his seed. The man sowed some along the path and it was trampled underfoot and devoured by birds. Some fell on the rock and grew up, but then withered away. Other seed fell among the thorns, and the thorns grew with it and choked the life out of the plants. And the last seed was sown into good soil. This seed grew and thrived, yielding much fruit. Jesus explains the parable to His disciples:

"Now the parable is this: The seed is the word of God. The ones along the path are those who have heard; then the devil comes and takes away the word from their hearts, so that they may not believe and be saved. And the ones on the rock are those who, when they hear the word, receive it with joy. But these have no root; they believe for a while, and in time of testing fall away. And as for what fell among the thorns, they are those who hear; but as they go on their way they are choked by the cares and riches and pleasures of life, and their fruit does not mature. As for that in the good soil, they are those who, hearing the word, hold it fast in an honest and good heart, and bear fruit with patience." Luke 8:11-15 ESV

When seeking God's wisdom, we should always "check our soil" to be sure His Word will be planted in fertile ground. Having good soil means we are primed and ready to align ourselves with God's standards. We are willing to obey Him no matter the cost. A woman with good soil will set aside her own opinions, perspectives, and preconceived notions and allow God's Word to transform her mind. She will apply His wisdom to her daily life. Her "roots" of faith will go down deep and form the foundation for her life. She will not be preoccupied or distracted by the allure of this world, for her heart will be set on eternity. When we become this woman, the woman we were created to be, God's wisdom will bloom and grow in our hearts and throughout our lives. We will know how to handle anything that comes our way, because our wisdom will come from above.

Blessed is the one who finds wisdom, and the one who gets understanding, for the gain from her {wisdom} is better than gain from silver and her profit better than gold. She is more precious than jewels, and nothing you desire can compare with her. Proverbs 3:12-15 ESV

One area of my life where I constantly need God's wisdom is in my parenting. As a parent of a toddler and a teenager, I face a lot of challenges that honestly I am ill equipped to handle on my own. Trying to figure out why my boys are acting the way they are sometimes leaves me baffled. Trying to control my own reactions and not take things so personal is a struggle. Instead of losing my cool and yelling, I am learning to stop and ask God for wisdom on how to handle a situation. I'm asking Him for the deeper reason why my child is acting the way they are acting, and how I can apply His wisdom in a graceful way that will bring about growth in my child.

With my youngest, I am learning to stop when I start to feel worked up about his behavior and ask God for His help not only to control my emotions, but to guide me towards the best way to handle the situation. With my oldest, I need God's wisdom in navigating the teenage world and everything that comes with it. With both boys I need to consistently ask God for wisdom on how *I* can grow as a parent and a Christ follower. Leaning on my own understanding brings chaos. Looking to God for wisdom facilitates peace. His ways are unbelievably higher than my own.

"For my thoughts are not your thoughts, neither are your ways my ways," declares the Lord. "As the heavens are higher than the earth, so are my ways higher than your ways and my thoughts than your thoughts." Isaiah 55:8-9 ESV

Sometimes, as in these situations with my boys, God's wisdom is instant. His guidance comes immediately by bringing an applicable Scripture to mind or by the Holy Spirit's gentle whisper of instruction in my thoughts. Other times though, seeking God's wisdom for a particular situation means I need to wait on His direction and not rush ahead with my own plans. It's not act first, seek God later but rather, seek His guidance before I act at all. In these moments, I learn to be still and patiently wait for Him to lead. He always comes through. He is faithful to me just as He will be faithful to you. He is ready and waiting to guide us all.

As we commit ourselves to Scripture reading, God's wisdom will implant in our souls. As we seek Him in prayer, He will guide our steps. When we are confused on how to handle our circumstances, He will be there to lead us. His incredible wisdom will be a light to our paths. When we are unable, He is able. We simply must seek Him and be committed to following His lead.

Personal Reflection:
Where do I typically look for wisdom? Do I trust in my own insight and opinion? Do I look to culture for answers?

Is God's Word my final authority? Do I trust that God knows best? Do I take the time to read His word and seek Him for guidance?

Is there a specific area of my life where I am not looking to God for wisdom but instead leaning on my own understanding? How can I realign my perspective with His and seek the wisdom from above?

Heavenly Father, we praise You as the Creator of all things and the holder of infinite knowledge. You and You alone know best. Your ways are higher than our own and we thank You for the glorious wisdom You provide. Thank for Your Word, which promises to lead us when we put You first and seek You above all else. We know Your promises are always true and You will never let us down. We are so grateful You know us and are concerned with every intimate detail of our lives. You are waiting to guide us and illuminate our paths. You are a good, good Father. We pray for Your help to become women who seek Your wisdom in all areas of our lives. Equip us with your wisdom to handle whatever comes our way. Give us wisdom in all our decisions. Give us wisdom in our parenting; we know we can't do it without You. Give us wisdom in our relationships; guide us into Your will so You can be most glorified. Lead us with Your wisdom down the paths You have already marked out for us. May Your word be our constant source of truth, may we look to it to guide our decisions. Reveal to us any area where we are relying on our own wisdom instead of Yours, and help us to realign our lives to Your will. In Jesus Holy name, Amen.

Chapter 21
Created to Shine

Her children rise up and call her blessed; her husband also, and he praises her. "Many women have done excellently, but you surpass them all." Proverbs 31:28-29 ESV

Give her the fruit of her hands and let her works praise her in the gates. Proverbs 31:31 ESV

A woman who recognizes and obeys God's calling on her life will be rewarded in many ways. She will be praised for her hard work and her God- honoring lifestyle. Her family will celebrate her excellence, and she will reap the blessings of the good seeds she has sown. As she seeks God, His grace will empower her to obey His Word and she will see the result of that obedient living all throughout her household.

Over the years as I've put God first, studying His Word consistently and applying it to my life, I have seen the amazing impact it has made not only personally, but in the lives of many others. God has answered countless prayers through my obedience. I can attest to the fact that life works better when we follow the Bible!

When we love God, we will obey Him. We will become a vessel through which His blessings and goodness can flow. First to us, and then through us. Our obedience to God will affect everyone around us. I've experienced this in the most beautiful way as I have watched God transform my husband's heart. This only began to happen once I dedicated myself to becoming the excellent wife God has called me to be. Instead of fixating on all the things I thought were wrong with my husband, (his lack of faith at the top of the list) I began to focus on myself. I realized that I couldn't control him, but I was responsible for my own obedience to God.

Nagging, controlling, and negativity towards my husband was not God's will for my life. I stopped focusing on him and all the things I thought *he* could be doing better and instead diligently began to apply God's Word to myself. Once I began to do this, the most amazing thing happened! My husband's heart began softening towards Jesus and I can happily say that He is now a follower of Christ!! The rewards that come from obedience are endless. When we know God's Word and we do His will, we will be blessed.

But the one who looks into the perfect law, the law of liberty, and perseveres, being no hearer who forgets but a doer who acts, he will be blessed in his doing. James 1:25 ESV

As God pours His blessings upon us and we begin to receive praise for our good deeds, humility is of utmost importance. A humble woman knows every good thing in her life is due to God's Spirit at work. It's natural to want to take credit for our own accomplishments, but we must give credit where credit is due. When we maintain a spirit of humility, not storing up praise in our own hearts but instead deflecting it to God, the honor goes where it belongs. It is the Holy Spirit who works in us and produces good. This puts boasting in its place.

What do you have that you did not receive? If then you received it, why do you boast as if you did not receive it? 1 Corinthians 4:7b ESV

So that, as it is written, "Let the one who boasts, boast in the Lord." 1 Corinthians 1:31 ESV

Pride is a sneaky thing. It will creep up and insist that all the praise rightfully belongs to us. It will blind us to the fact that God alone deserves all the glory. Pride puffs up, but humility keeps the focus where it belongs. On God, not us. God detests pride. Scripture goes so far as to say He *opposes* the prideful. Any prideful thoughts need to be addressed immediately. When pride starts to bubble up in our souls, we need to swiftly identify it, confess it, and ask God to remove it. Remembering how far God has brought us helps keep pride in check. Keeping ourselves humble means God won't have to do the humbling for us (not a fun experience). Humility is precious in the eyes of the Lord.

*Clothe yourselves, all of you, with humility toward one another, for God opposes the proud but gives grace to the humble. Humble yourselves, therefore, under the mighty hand of God so that at the proper time He may exalt you.
1 Peter 5:5a-6 ESV*

God's glory will become visible in our actions when we commit to becoming the women He created us to be. Through us, others will be able to experience His goodness in a tangible way. As we go back to the concept of praise, Scripture reveals something very interesting. The Hebrew word used for praise was *halal*, which was a verb that had multiple meanings. It meant to celebrate and commend, which is what we understand this word to mean today. Yet, it also meant to shine; to give off or reflect light.

Light is used many times in Scripture to symbolize God, faith, and holiness. I just love this depiction! When we live the lives we were created to live by committing ourselves to excellence and righteous living, our good deeds will shine with the light of Jesus. We will reflect His loving character to a desperate world.

When Jesus spoke again to the people, he said, "I am the light of the world. Whoever follows me will never walk in darkness, but will have the light of life." John 8:12 ESV

Jesus radiated light the entire time He walked this Earth. His brilliant words spoken atop mountains penetrated the hearts and souls of those listening. His words illuminated the character of God, and the intent behind His laws. His light blazed fiercely against sin, yet was a warm and glowing ember of hope towards sinners. The healing power of Jesus' light restored lepers, healed the sick, raised the dead, and brought sight to the blind. The darkness trembled as He cast out demons and freed the oppressed.

The Pharisees sought to extinguish Jesus as they nailed Him to the cross, yet it was impossible for His light to be snuffed out. Jesus rose again in all His dazzling glory to conquer death once and for all. Then He infused His disciples with the light of His Holy Spirit, and commanded them to take that light to everyone in the world. His light still exists today, through each and every one of His followers. He tells us to shine this light brightly for all to see.

"You are the light of the world. A city set on a hill cannot be hidden. Nor do people light a lamp and put it under a basket, but on a stand, and it gives light to all in the house." Matthew 5:14-15 ESV

Jesus came into the world as a shining light to conquer evil and push back the darkness. As His followers, we were created to do the same. We are commanded to put on the armor of light and walk as children of light. We are asked to shine for Him and reflect His brilliance to all. Our faithfulness, love, and integrity reflect the light of Jesus for all to see. As we persist in good deeds, empowered by the Holy Spirit, others will be drawn to the true light of Christ. As we follow the example of Jesus, we will carry His light to those who are still walking in darkness.

Just as plants need light to survive physically, every one of us needs the light of Jesus to survive spiritually. There is only spiritual darkness until Jesus lights up our life with His glorious presence. We step out of the shadows and into His warm and comforting light when we receive Him as Lord and Savior. He shines His light into the dark places of our lives and exposes them to bring growth and healing. He illuminates our sin to guide us into repentance and then He empowers us with grace to change. His light saves, restores, guides, and revives.

The people who walked in darkness have seen a great light; those who dwelt in a land of deep darkness, on them has light shone. Isaiah 9:2 ESV

Because our eyes have been so wonderfully designed by our Creator, they will adjust to our surroundings. The sensitivity of our retinas will either increase or decrease based upon whether we are going from dark to light or vice versa. Reflexive changes will occur in our pupils and retinal neurons will rapidly adapt. After about 30 – 45 minutes in the dark we will be able to see well.

I picture my life before Christ as being in a dark room. I had been there for a long time and my eyes had fully adjusted. I was comfortable there. I was even under the delusion that I could see everything perfectly clearly. I had no clue that Jesus waited in the darkness as the door that would usher me into the warm sunlight.

I was in the dark for so long; I didn't even realize there was something brilliant waiting for me on the other side of that door. At first, the light dazzled my eyes as I left the shadows. Yet, before long, I had adjusted; and today I couldn't imagine going back to the darkness. Isn't it crazy how we don't realize we are walking in darkness until it is revealed to us? It is only after Jesus brings us into the light that our spiritual eyes are opened and we begin to see everything crystal clear.

Just as the leaves of a plant will grow towards the sunlight, we will begin to gravitate towards the things of Jesus, such as prayer, Bible reading, and spending time with other believers. We will steer clear of things associated with darkness and evil.

"And this is the judgment: the light has come into the world, and people loved the darkness rather than the light because their works were evil. For everyone who does wicked things hates the light and does not come to the light, lest his works should be exposed. But whoever does what is true comes to the light, so that it may be clearly seen that his works have been carried out in God." John 3:19-21 ESV

When we commit ourselves to excellence we will carry the light of Jesus everywhere we go. This light will illuminate everything. It will bring warmth to our households and to others. It will dispel the darkness that threatens to envelop our very existence. It will invite praise, which will then be an opportunity to glorify our Heavenly Father, from whom all blessings flow.

"In the same way, let your light shine before others, so that they may see your good works and give glory to your Father who is in heaven." Matthew 5:16 ESV

Personal Reflection:

Has my commitment to living life God's way resulted in blessings not only for myself, but for those around me? What positive changes has my faith made in my life as I've applied God's Word? Spend some time recounting God's faithfulness in this area.

Do I recognize God as the giver of all good things in my life? Am I giving God the credit and the glory for the praise I receive? Do I struggle with prideful thoughts? If so, how can I maintain a spirit of humility?

Am I conscious of reflecting Jesus' light to others? Am I intentional about bringing His light into the dark places not only in my own life but into the lives of other people?

Heavenly Father, we praise Your Holy name and thank You for Your Word today. We are so grateful for the blessings that obedience brings. We thank You that our children call us blessed and our husbands praise us, for we know it is because of Your Spirit at work in our lives. We pray You will keep us walking in love and obedience to You, and continue to reveal to us the areas where we fall short. Forgive us for any prideful thoughts or attitudes. We know how much You hate pride and we pray You would continue to cultivate humble hearts in each and every one of us. Thank You for the light of Jesus which shines brightly in our hearts. We ask for You to shine Your light into all of the dark places in our lives, exposing sin and bringing healing to our souls. Equip us to be light-bearers in this dark world, illuminating the true path to eternity with You, and bringing the hope of Jesus to all. As we push back the darkness with the light of Your Spirit, may all come to know You and glorify Your precious name. In Jesus name, Amen.

Chapter 22

Created to Fear God

Charm is deceitful and beauty is vain, but a woman who fears the Lord is to be praised. Proverbs 31:30 ESV

We were designed to be women who would possess a healthy fear of the Lord. Fear of the Lord is something that society tends to ignore. Yet, because Scripture mentions this 72 times, we would be wise to open our hearts to receive this word. The Bible tells us to love God with everything that is in us. Yet, it also commands us to fear Him. Love for the Lord and fear of the Lord go hand in hand.

The Hebrew word used for fear was *yare*, which signified an awe-inspiring, respectful admiration of God's majesty. Strong's concordance says this about the word *yare*: "People who feared God were considered faithful and trustworthy, for such fear constrained them to believe and act morally." Those who feared God kept His laws. Their lives reflected their respect for God's authority. We were created to possess this same respect for God.

"Oh that they had such a heart as this always, to fear me and to keep all my commandments, that it might go well with them and with their descendants forever!"
Deuteronomy 5:29 ESV

The concept of fearing God is very easy to misunderstand, and we must be careful to interpret it the right way. Martin Luther, the great theologian and Protestant Reformer, explained this best. He contrasted two types of fear. The first, *servile* fear, can be described as a dreadful anxiety towards another person. This would be similar to the fear a prisoner in a torture chamber would have towards his tormentor.

Secondly there is *filail* fear, which derives from the Latin concept of family. This type of fear can best be described as fear of offending the ones we love and respect. It is similar to the healthy fear children should have towards their parents, their authority figures. This is the type of fear we should feel toward God. We should not be scared of Him, but we should fear disobeying because we love and respect Him so much. It is this healthy fear that leads to obedience and a life that brings honor to God.

Now therefore fear the Lord and serve Him in sincerity and in faithfulness. Joshua 24:14 ESV

We were designed to love God with all of our hearts, minds, and souls. When we possess this type of love for God we will desire to please Him. We will want to be obedient. A healthy fear of the Lord means we will recognize His authority and take Him at His word when He speaks. This fear will move us to obedience.

We see this concept played out during the exodus of the Israelites from the land of Egypt. God warned His people that He would be sending a plague of hail down upon their land, a consequence of Pharaoh's refusal to let the Israelites go. He told His people to bring their animals and families out from the field and into shelter, so they would be protected from the deadly hail. Scripture shows us the difference between those who feared God and those who did not.

Then whoever feared the word of the Lord among the servants of Pharaoh made his servants and his livestock flee to the houses. But he who did not regard the word of the Lord left his servants and his livestock in the field. Exodus 9:20-21 NKJV

As you can imagine, God did exactly as He said He would do. He rained down the heaviest hail the nation of Egypt had ever seen. Those who feared God believed He would do what He said He would do, and acted accordingly. They remained safe. The others, those who disregarded His Word, not so much. God spoke with authority those thousands of years ago, and the wise people listened.

His Word still carries the same weight of that authority today. We are called to fear Him, respect Him, and live our lives in obedience to His will. Because we love Him. Because we honor His Word and His supremacy over all. Because we fear disobeying Him and we fear His discipline. God disciplines those He loves, just as a father disciplines his own children. This discipline leads us away from sin and towards righteousness. Again in Scripture we see the correlation between fear/discipline, and a parent's authority.

It is for discipline that you have to endure. God is treating you as sons. For what son is there whom his father does not discipline?... Besides this, we have had earthly fathers who disciplined us and we respected them... For they disciplined us for a short time as it seemed best to them, but He disciplines us for our good, that we may share His holiness. For the moment all discipline seems painful rather than pleasant, but later it yields the peaceful fruit of righteousness to those who have been trained by it. Hebrews 12:7,9a-11 ESV

The writer of Hebrews continues on and instructs believers to strive for peace and holiness. He commands us to avoid bitterness and sexual immorality. These behaviors (or lack thereof) reflect a healthy fear of the Lord and will help us to avoid provoking His discipline. We see the striking similarities between this passage and the relationship between parent and child. Since God is our authority, we will avoid doing things He tells us not to do. We will love what He loves and hate what He hates.

When He disciplines us, we will not harden our hearts towards sin. Instead we will accept His discipline, repent, and move forward towards right living, with the help of the Holy Spirit.

Blessed is the one who fears the Lord always, but whoever hardens his heart will fall into calamity. Proverbs 28:14 ESV

In my own life, I didn't have a solid understanding of God's authority until I dedicated myself to reading the entire Old Testament. Even though we are under a new covenant with Jesus, and not bound by specific laws given to the Israelites, reading the Old Testament is still foundational to our faith. The Old Testament gives us a complete picture of God's character, shows us how He relates to His people, and explains why we so desperately need a Savior. Reading the Old Testament instilled in me a deep awareness of two attributes of God that we tend to shy away from discussing: His holiness and His wrath.

It is tempting to want to focus only on the loving aspects of God's character, and there are so many of those! His love, grace, compassion, and kindness. His patience, gentleness, and tenderness. These qualities are wonderful and so necessary to ponder upon, yet they are only a portion of God's character. He is also a fierce God of justice and vengeance. He embodies wrath against sin and disobedience. He is Holy. He is the God who caused the great prophet Isaiah, after seeing Him in a vision, to declare:

"Woe is me! For I am lost; for I am a man of unclean lips, and I dwell in the midst of a people of unclean lips; for my eyes have seen the King, the Lord of hosts!" Isaiah 6:5 ESV

Our God cannot be approached in a flippant manner. We must remember that though Scripture says He is our Abba (Daddy) Father, He is also holy and worthy of every ounce of reverence we can muster. The God of the Bible commands respect. This is very different from the popular concept many have of God today, a big teddy bear in the sky just waiting to sprinkle blessings upon us and welcome everyone into heaven. This god is void of authority, commands no respect, and incites zero motivation to live a righteous life marked by obedience and surrender. Culture's god stands in stark contrast to how the true God is described biblically, even in the New Testament.

Therefore let us be grateful for receiving a kingdom that cannot be shaken, and thus let us offer to God acceptable worship, with reverence and awe, for our God is a consuming fire. Hebrews 12:26 ESV

Our God is a consuming fire. We were designed to be women who would worship Him with reverence and awe. Another important (and seldom mentioned) aspect of God's character is His jealousy. Typically we view jealousy as something negative, and in most contexts it is. However, when we refer to God's jealousy, we are not speaking of the sinful envy that we tend to feel as humans. God's jealousy is based on His love and concern for us. He is jealous for our love, our affection, and our devotion. He is jealous to be first place in our lives with no other idols before Him, which He rightly deserves.

In the Old Testament, Moses spoke of God's jealousy and how the Israelites had provoked it. God created the Israelites.

He established them and brought them out of slavery. He cared for them, provided for their needs, and guided their paths. Yet the Israelites still chose to turn away from the true God and instead worship false gods. They forgot all about their Maker, which stirred God's jealousy and kindled His anger.

This story is referred to again in the New Testament when Paul uses it to instruct the believers in Corinth, and his instruction applies to us today as well. Paul recounts the story of the Israelites and their idolatry as an example for us *not* to follow. He tells us not to indulge in sinful pleasures. To flee from idolatry. He equates idolatry (literal or figurative worship of false gods) as being a participant with demons.

I do not want you to be participants with demons. You cannot drink the cup of the Lord and the cup of demons. You cannot partake of the table of the Lord and the table of demons. Shall we provoke the Lord to jealousy? Are we stronger than He?
1 Corinthians 10:20b-22 ESV

So how can we make sure we are not stirring God's jealousy by partaking at the table of demons? Obviously we are not literally sitting down with demons, yet we must realize there are spiritual implications to everything. In this day and age it's very common for someone to have a buffet of religious beliefs. Honestly, most of us don't know any better. Our society is full of people who want to be "spiritual but not religious". Without a full knowledge of the Bible, it can be difficult to discern what is okay and what isn't.

The Bible says there is a way that seems right to us, but in the end it leads to death (Proverbs 14:12). Many of the activities popular today are deeply rooted in false religions. Some, like astrology and the seeking of mediums and psychics, are even specifically mentioned (and forbidden) in the Bible. Others, like Reiki healing and yoga, have deep roots in other religions. At its core, yoga was designed to pay homage to, and become one with, the false gods of Hinduism. The very word, *yoga*, means to unite.

Many of these practices are encompassed in the New Age movement, which takes advantage of a person's innate desire for a deep spiritual life. Many are deceived into believing these are good, beneficial practices that can actually lead to a closer relationship with the Lord. They do not realize that these practices stand in stark opposition to the Bible. These practices are heavily entwined with demonic principles and involving ourselves with them opens us up to spiritual darkness and incites God's jealousy.

They stirred him to jealousy with strange gods; with abominations they provoked him to anger.
Deuteronomy 32:16 ESV

Idolatry in any form provokes God's anger and sparks His jealousy for our affections. Aside from being aware of the spiritual implications of our activities, and whether or not they are in alignment with the Bible, we should also be diligent in removing idols from our lives. Idols come in many forms. We can idolize success, relationships, celebrities, money, even our own physical image. We idolize these things when we give them the devotion that rightly belongs to God. When pursuit of them takes precedence over our pursuit of God, we are in danger of provoking His jealousy.

In 627 BC, the prophet Jeremiah shared God's very words with the Israelites. Through his message we see a glimpse of God's heart and we receive a clear picture of how He feels when we turn to idols and false gods. Jeremiah recounted to the Israelites how God remembered their devotion and love in the beginning. The people had followed Him wholeheartedly and walked in close relationship and obedience to Him. They knew God personally and they were known by God. God provided daily sustenance and constant guidance, yet eventually the Israelites rejected Him. They turned away from Him, the never-ending source of physical and spiritual nourishment, for idols. They sinned against the Lord and, perhaps worst of all, Scripture says they did not know Him any longer.

The Hebrew word used for know was *yada*, which gave the idea of deep intimacy. It signified closeness and companionship. It gave the impression of a complete connection to the heart of another. In fact, this word was also used when describing the physical love shared between a husband and wife. The Israelites abandoned this beautiful relationship with the Lord and instead chose idolatry. Isn't that sad?

Perhaps this was why Jeremiah was known as the weeping prophet. To see how far Israel had strayed from God and then to have to relay God's own sadness and anger at their rebellion must have broken the prophet's heart. I'm sure Jeremiah also wept to see the destruction the Israelites had brought upon themselves for turning away from God and provoking His anger.

"For my people have committed two evils: they have forsaken me, the fountain of living waters, and hewed out cisterns for themselves, broken cisterns that can hold no water."
Jeremiah 2:13 ESV

When we see how much idol worship hurts God's heart and provokes His jealousy, it lights a fire in us to take the necessary steps to remove it from our lives. A healthy fear of God will lead to proper worship. As we get to know Him through His Word, Old Testament and New, we will begin to worship Him as He truly is, not merely who we perceive Him to be. False beliefs about His character will fall away.

When we stumble across something in the Bible that we don't understand about God, the best thing we can do is to pray for Him to answer any questions we might have. Whenever I struggle with a particular Scripture and ask for understanding, God always guides me to the truth. He reveals Himself in a deeper way and broadens my perception.

While we never want to undermine the aspects of God's character discussed today, we must be careful not to go too far in that direction either. We need a healthy balance. While some churches put too much emphasis on God's love and grace, thereby leading to a skewed view of God not conducive to personal holiness, others go overboard on preaching about God's wrath and they scare people away. We must remember; God is both. Love and Wrath. Relational and Holy. Grace and Truth.

Jesus was the visible image of the invisible God and the perfect balance of grace and truth. He extended His love, kindness, and compassion wherever He went, but He also spoke firmly on sin. He pointed out the hypocrisy of people's hearts and encouraged them towards righteous living; yet He also served others, healed their illnesses, and forgave their sins. He warned of the dangers of hell; yet at the same time, made a way for each and every one of us to be welcomed into heaven with open arms. May we praise God daily for every aspect of His multi-faceted, amazing character, and seek to live our lives in reverence and awe of His Mighty Name.

But the Lord takes pleasure in those who fear Him, in those who hope in His steadfast love. Psalm 147:11 ESV

Personal Reflection:
Do I possess a healthy fear of the Lord? Do I revere Him and respect His authority? Do I fear disobeying Him and being disciplined by Him?

Is there an area of habitual sin in my life where I have disregarded God's authority?

Are their idols in my life that are taking God's place?
Have I involved myself in any way with practices that are tied to the worship of other religions or forbidden biblically?

Heavenly Father, we praise Your Holy name. We approach You in reverent awe and wonder at Your majesty. No-one is greater than You. You are worthy of every ounce of our admiration and praise. Thank You for revealing Yourself so clearly to us in Scripture. Please forgive us for the times we have not given You the respect You deserve. Help us to recognize Your authority and to be willing to live under that authority. Where healthy fear is lacking, give us a deeper understanding of Your character. Give us the wisdom and the desire to honor and obey You. Reveal to us any areas of sin and disobedience in our lives. We pray we will always follow You whole-heartedly, that our devotion would remain steadfast. Reveal to us any personal idols that we have placed above you. Forgive us for worshipping anyone or anything in place of You. We ask that You reveal to us any area where we have knowingly or unknowingly been participants with demons by involving ourselves in the practices of other religions, or activities that dishonor You. We ask Your forgiveness for this and we renounce any involvement in these activities. Please close any spiritual doors we have opened that have allowed spiritual darkness or demonic interference into our lives. May we worship You, and You only, always in spirit and in truth. We pray this in Jesus name, the Name above all Names. Amen

Chapter 23
Created to be Gracious

A gracious woman gets honor...
Proverbs 11:16a ESV

Gracious: Showing divine grace.

We were designed to be women who would reflect the grace of God in all that we do. Because of this, others will hold us in high esteem, but even more importantly; God will be honored. There is nothing more amazing than the grace of God. His grace seeks us out, redeems, and restores. It empowers us to live righteously. It covers our sin and awakens our souls to His love. Grace is the reason we live and the reason we have a relationship with the Almighty Father.

Grace gives us the chance to push the reset button and start again. Grace picks us up when we are at our lowest, in the midst of our deepest failures, and whispers forgiveness and encouragement into our souls. It enables a great exchange: our guilt and shame for God's peace and victory. Where would we be without it? God is so good. His mercies never end, and His grace is freely given to those who seek Him.

Seek the Lord while He may be found; call upon Him while He is near; let the wicked forsake His way, and the unrighteous man his thoughts; let him return to the Lord, that He may have compassion on him, and to our God, for He will abundantly pardon. Isaiah 55:6-7 ESV

Before we even had a thought in our minds to follow Jesus, grace was busy drawing us in. This just astounds me every time I think of it. It is truly incredible and such a reflection of God's heart towards us. He seeks us out because we are precious to Him. We are valuable. We are His creation, His daughters. He has always desired to live in close relationship with His creation, from now into eternity. And He will chase us down and draw us in with His precious grace until we desire that relationship just as much as He.

My favorite depiction of this is found in the parable of the Prodigal Son. Jesus tells this parable to illustrate our relationship with God, and it speaks volumes to me personally because I was once this prodigal. I was far from God. I did horribly sinful things, a reflection of my lost soul. Yet, His grace fought until I was found.

There was a man who had two sons. The youngest came to his father and asked for his share of the inheritance, which his father gladly gave. The son then traveled to a far away country and squandered everything in reckless and wild living. He was left with nothing, and when a famine arose in the land he took a job feeding pigs. Hungry and guilt-ridden, he would rather sleep and eat with pigs than return home and admit his failure.

Finally one day he came to his senses and realized he must go home. He knew he was wrong. He had every intention of admitting his guilt and humbly accepting whatever punishment his sins would bring. He hung his head in shame as he approached his father's house. Yet, things didn't go the way he thought they would. The unexpected reaction he received is but a snapshot of our Heavenly Father's reaction when we "return home".

"And he arose and came to his father. But while he was still a long way off, his father saw him and felt compassion, and ran and embraced him and kissed him. And the son said to him, 'Father, I have sinned against heaven and before you. I am no longer worthy to be called your son.' But the father said to his servants, 'Bring quickly the best robe, and put it on him, and put a ring on his hand, and shoes on his feet. And bring the fattened calf and kill it, and let us eat and celebrate. For this my son was dead, and is alive again; he was lost, and is found.' And they began to celebrate." Luke 15:20-24 ESV

Not only did the prodigal son's father forgive him, he bestowed upon him the best robe and the fattiest calf. He threw the biggest celebration likely his household had ever seen. I love the original Greek word for lost used in this passage. The word was *apollumi,* and it signified something of value that had been lost to its owner. It also referred to those who wander away. Just as this son belonged to his father; we belong to our Heavenly Father. When we wander away from Him, He will stop at nothing to find us.

The Scripture says while the son was still a long way off, his father ran to meet him and embraced him compassionately. Our Father in Heaven does the same for us. When we are far from Him, when we are lost, when we wander; He has compassion on us. He runs to us, meets us with the cross of Christ, and wraps us in His warm embrace of grace. He pours that undeserved grace over our lives, and redirects our paths. And when we return to Him, all of Heaven celebrates!

"Just so, I tell you, there will be more joy in heaven over one sinner who repents than over ninety-nine righteous persons who need no repentance." Luke 15:7 ESV

God's mercies never fail. His grace is unbelievably sufficient. It is available for everybody, even the most hardened of sinners. Not only does His grace find us when we are lost, it continually forgives and empowers us as we journey with Christ. Every failure is a fresh opportunity to experience God's grace in a powerful way. See, we will never follow Jesus perfectly. Try as we might, our sinful nature will always get in the way. We will struggle. We will feel like we've failed God. We will feel unworthy of His love. The important thing to remember in these moments of defeat and discouragement is to allow our failures to push us closer *to* God, not further away.

So often, when we feel like we've blown it, we want to hide from God. Our guilt convinces us that God wants nothing to do with us, and we feel too defeated to even pray. Feelings of shame and inadequacy envelop our souls. In these moments the enemy has us exactly where he wants us. He starts in with his lies. "You will never change," he says. "It's no use. You may as well just give up on trying to live a life that pleases God." Does any of this sound familiar? These are tough moments, and I have had my fair share of them. Yet, grace is there waiting. It is waiting to forgive, to heal, to give us a chance to pick up the pieces and start again. We are always one heartfelt prayer away from restoration.

The enemy would love to keep us in a place of blame and shame, guilt and grief. He heaps condemnation upon our heads to keep us discouraged and render us ineffective in God's kingdom. This is why it's so important to know the difference between conviction and condemnation. Conviction comes from the Holy Spirit. It is used by God to make us aware of our sin so we will repent and pursue righteous living. Conviction is a necessary part of our sanctification. It may not always be the most comfortable thing, but it is a good thing.

Conviction is a sign of God's Spirit at work in us. Conviction always carries with it the hope of restoration, and points us to God's grace.

On the flip side, there is condemnation. Condemnation is hate-filled and hopeless. There is no promise of grace, only judgment. Condemnation swallows us up with thoughts of failure and shame, and there is no clear way out. This comes straight from the devil. Condemnation will never come from God. Only conviction.

There is therefore now no condemnation for those who are in Christ Jesus. Romans 8:1 ESV

So, when you do fail, as you are bound to do, remember this: do not listen to the lies of the enemy! Throw yourself on the mercy of God, receive His grace and move forward in obedience. One thing that has been so helpful to me is realizing God already knows every single one of the mistakes I will make and He loves me anyway. He will continue to finish what He started in my life because I belong to Him. He sees the bigger picture, and knows every hill and valley along the way. He is well aware of my weaknesses, yet His grace is enough to sustain me and grow me into the woman He created me to be.

Nowhere in the Scriptures is this truth more evident than in Peter's story. I just love Peter, probably because I can really relate to Him as a person. Bold. Impulsive. Kind of a know it all. On the fateful night of Jesus' arrest, during His last supper, He told His disciples that each one of them would desert Him that very night. To which Peter brazenly responded, "Even if all fall away on account of you, I never will." (Matthew 26:33.)

Jesus then startled him with this news: not only would Peter fall away, but before the rooster crowed that very night, Peter would deny Him three times. True to the word, that same night after Jesus' arrest, all of Peter's boldness suddenly disappeared. He denied knowing Jesus; once, twice, and at the third denial the rooster crowed. When he heard this sound, Peter remembered the words of His Lord and the Scripture says he wept bitterly.

Have you ever felt like Peter? I know I have. Promises to God: broken. Vows to change: ruined. Again. I felt this way just the very week I wrote this chapter. All of my good intentions to be less reactive and more patient with my children had gone down the drain as I lost my temper and yelled, acting in a way I know I never should. Shame reared its ugly head and bitterness overwhelmed my soul. Yet, because of grace, I knew I didn't have to stay in that place. Failure isn't the end of Peter's story and failure isn't the end of mine either. Or yours.

Let's move on, past the resurrection of Jesus. Peter was fishing with some of the other disciples on their boat. I imagine he couldn't get his failure out of his mind, replaying his denial over and over and drowning in regret. Suddenly, Jesus appeared on the shore! How did Peter react? Did he hang his head in shame and defeat or did he embrace God's forgiveness and mercy?

That disciple whom Jesus loved therefore said to Peter, "It is the Lord!" When Simon Peter heard that it was the Lord, he put on his outer garment, for he was stripped for work, and threw himself into the sea. John 21:7 ESV

What a beautiful picture of how we should respond after failure. Running to God with everything we have. Throwing ourselves at His mercy and asking for a chance to start again. Seeking out His grace, which He waits to bestow abundantly upon us. Every day is a chance to start again. God continually reminds us of this all throughout Scripture.

On tough days, when I feel particularly defeated and the enemy tries to overcome my mind with his lies, grace swoops in and reminds me that God never gives up on me. He will continue to lead me and guide me into His will for my life. He will continue to bring good and He will never give up on me. His love is unwavering and His mercies are unending.

But this I call to mind, and therefore I have hope: The steadfast love of the Lord never ceases; His mercies never come to an end; they are new every morning; great is your faithfulness. Lamentations 3:21-24 ESV

God's grace not only forgave Peter and washed his sins away, it empowered him to continue on and live the life he was created to live; a life marked by obedience and righteousness. Grace smoothed out Peter's rough edges. It turned Him into a godly man and a pioneer in the faith. Grace changes lives. It changed Peter's. It changed mine. And it will change yours as well.

As we receive this grace, let us remember to give to others that which we have been so abundantly given. We were created to be conduits of God's amazing grace so let us be women whose lives overflow with an abundance of gracious actions. May we seek out others to bestow kindness upon. May we breathe God's grace into every situation and every conversation. May we forgive, love, and empower those around us. When we live the way we were designed to live, others will catch a glimpse of God's gracious heart and be drawn to His sweet love.

Gracious words are like a honeycomb, sweetness to the soul and health to the body. Proverbs 16:24 ESV

Personal Reflection:

What are some specific moments in my life that I have received God's grace? (Spend some time reflecting on these and thanking God for His amazing gift.)

Do I tend to run to God after failure or away? How can I change my patterns by applying what I learned about grace today? What specific Scriptures can I remind myself of when the enemy tries to condemn me?

Do I recognize the difference between condemnation and conviction? Does conviction lead me to change my behavior?

Do I give the same grace to others that I have received from God? Am I merciful and forgiving, allowing others room to make mistakes?

Heavenly Father, we come to You humbly today, just so grateful for Your amazing grace. You sought us out when we were lost. You brought us home and lavished Your love upon us. Your mercies know no end. As undeserving recipients of Your grace, all we can do is say thank You, and seek to live in gratitude for all You have done for us. May Your grace continually empower us to live righteously. May it continue to forgive us and reach us at our lowest points, offering us the chance to begin again. We pray against any scheme or plan of the enemy to beat us down with condemnation in moments of failure. We pray we would immediately recognize his tricks and shut them down. May our failures make us run to You, quick to confess and receive Your cleansing and forgiveness. Let us never use Your grace as an excuse to sin, but rather seek to live life Your way because we love You and want to please You. Keep us moving forward in obedience. Keep us near to You, and abiding in Your love. Remind us to give grace to others. As we have received Your mercy, let us always be merciful. May we draw others to You with our gracious words and actions. In Jesus mighty name, Amen.

Chapter 24
Created to be Beautiful

Do not let your adorning be external – the braiding of hair and the putting on of gold jewelry, or the clothing you wear – but let your adorning be the hidden person of the heart with the imperishable beauty of a gentle and quiet spirit, which in God's sight is very precious. 1 Peter 3:3-4 ESV

Each and every one of us has been created to cultivate inner beauty, which in the eyes of God is precious and valued. This message flies in the face of everything culture pushes us to be. Society tells us we must be beautiful on the outside, that our outer beauty determines our worth. The beauty industry is a 265 billion dollar a year business. Women go to great lengths to measure up to culture's standard of beauty.

Trendy hair and perfectly manicured nails. Smooth and wrinkle-free skin. Toned body and flattering designer clothes. The list goes on and on. According to market research, the average woman dedicates 335 hours a year on her appearance, and spends $3,756 a year on beauty-related goods and services. I think it's safe to say our culture is rather obsessed with beauty. Yet, a woman was not designed to look to culture to measure her worth. Instead, as she looks to her Creator, He will assign the value to her that she seeks.

For the Lord sees not as man sees: man looks on the outward appearance, but the Lord looks on the heart.
1 Samuel 16:7 ESV

What if we spent as much time cultivating beauty on the inside as we do the outside? What if, instead of caring so much about the image we project to others, what mattered most to us was how our hearts looked to God? All the effort we exert to look beautiful on the outside is not what God deems important. How He defines beauty is what truly matters. So what is God's definition of beauty? Scripture tells us that a beautiful woman is one with a gentle and quiet spirit. This is precious in His sight. Outer beauty is fleeting, temporary. Inner beauty is eternal. It never perishes. It is this beauty we should spend our time developing, the hidden person of the heart. Let's discuss a few of the words used in this Scripture so we can have a better picture of what this looks like.

The first word of significance in this passage is the word adorning. The original word used in the Greek language was the word *kosmos*, which signified an orderly arrangement or decoration. Essentially what this means is that we are to put everything in order internally rather than externally. We do this by investing primarily in our spiritual life, not prioritizing our physical beauty. It isn't wrong to want to look our best, but our focus should be on cultivating the inner beauty which God finds very precious. Our decoration, so to speak, should be on the inside. This beauty is personified with a gentle and quiet spirit.

I love the meaning of the word gentle in this passage. A gentle woman is one who is mild, humble, and meek, with a soothing disposition. I immediately think of Jesus when I hear this description. Jesus was humble and gentle. He was the epitome of meekness. In our culture, the word meek carries a negative connotation. We see a meek person as someone who is quiet and easily imposed upon, a pushover. However; this isn't what the Bible meant at all when it described meekness.

The Greek word for meek, translated from the words *praus/prautes*, meant humility, courtesy, and gentleness. From Strong's Concordance: "*Prautes*, according to Aristotle, is the middle standing between two extremes, getting angry without reason, and not getting angry at all. It is the result of a strong man's choice to control his reactions in submission to God. It is a balance born in strength of character, stemming from confident trust in God, not from weakness or fear."

Meekness is strength under control. This is an exact representation of how Jesus lived His life on Earth. He had all the Divine power in the universe at His disposal yet He chose to lay it all aside to fulfill the Father's plan. He could have called down legions of angels to obliterate His enemies as they beat Him, spit upon Him, and taunted Him. He could have destroyed the very cross they nailed Him to with one word. Nevertheless, He restrained His power for our benefit. He willingly chose to endure the humility and torture of the cross. Strength under control. A strong man's choice to control His reactions in submission to God. Jesus had a humble assessment of self and an unwavering confidence in the Father.

Jesus also demonstrated this gentle spirit when He refused to engage with those who would attempt to trap Him in His words or start an argument. He chose the gentle route every time, and when we do the same we reflect His character. A woman who cultivates inner beauty by meditating on and imitating the meekness of Jesus is seen as precious to the Lord. Her gentle spirit will be evident, and her life will bring God glory.

Let your gentleness be evident to all. The Lord is near.
Philippians 4:5 NIV

We reflect the gentle spirit of Jesus when, in humility, we put others first. When grace abounds in our hearts and our actions. When life becomes less about winning arguments and proving ourselves right, and more about being a peacemaker. This is absolutely an area where I am a work in progress. I love to be right. I have a burning desire to prove my point, to be understood and make others see things my way. Sometimes my desire to be right, and prove others wrong, wins over my desire to bring peace to a relationship and smooth over conflict.

Is it precious in God's eyes when I argue my point? Am I shining my inner beauty and gentle spirit for all to see when I refuse to listen to someone else's perspective, thinking I have it all figured out already? Certainly not. My attitude in these moments is anything but gentle. It is in these moments that I must make a conscious effort to stop and reel in my pride and my emotions. I must remind myself to be gracious and humble, to exude a gentle spirit and be a peacemaker. Honestly this is tough to do. However; the more time I spend filling myself with the things of God, nourishing my inner beauty by prioritizing my spiritual life, the easier it becomes.

"But seek first the kingdom of God and His righteousness, and all these things will be added to you." Matthew 6:33 ESV

The word quiet in the Greek signified an undisturbed and peaceful state. To be disturbed means to have our normal pattern or function disrupted. A woman with an undisturbed spirit is a woman who has her hope so fully set on God that nothing shakes her. A woman with a quiet spirit has a steady confidence in God and does not allow outside influence to disturb that confidence. She knows exactly who she belongs to. Her faith makes her fearless and bold. This truth really speaks to my soul. When I ponder the fact that strong faith and a peaceful spirit equals beauty in my Heavenly Father's eyes, it magnifies my connection to Him as His daughter.

When faith was spoken of in the Old Testament, the Hebrew language suggested this very same connection. The Hebrew word for believe was *aman* and it was a verb that meant: "To be firm, to support, nurture. That of providing stability and confidence, like a baby would find in the arms of a parent." Isn't that just beautiful? A baby in the arms of a parent doesn't worry about the storms of life. This baby knows she is secure and cared for by her loving caretaker. A baby expects that her parent will provide, and she knows she is loved. She is undisturbed, peaceful; safe in her parent's care.

This is the faith God asks of us, the hope we have which is precious and valued in His eyes. As we nurture our faith by focusing on God and allowing Him to transform the inner person of the heart, a tranquil spirit will result. The trials of life will not disturb our peace, because our confidence will rest in our Heavenly Father.

So we do not lose heart. Though our outer self is wasting away, our inner self is being renewed day by day. For this light momentary affliction is preparing for us an eternal weight of glory beyond all comparison, as we look not to the things that are seen but to the things that are unseen. For the things that are seen are transient, but the things that are unseen are eternal. 2 Corinthians 4:16-18 ESV

Now that we have a clear understanding of what constitutes beauty in God's eyes we can begin to shift our focus from outward beauty to inward. We can implement the necessary steps to cultivate this gentle and quiet spirit as we remind ourselves to seek God's approval, not man's. We can stop looking to society to define beauty, and instead look to God's Word.

The outward expression of this inward heart change will manifest itself in the way we dress and present ourselves. A woman that desires to please God will also make an effort to dress in a way that will honor Him. As she begins to evaluate her worth in how God sees her, she won't need to look for validation from others.

She will begin to see herself differently, with respect, and adjust her outward appearance to reflect her faith.

Likewise also that women should adorn themselves in respectable apparel, with modesty and self control, not with braided hair and gold or pearls or costly attire, but with what is proper for women who profess godliness –with good works.
1 Timothy 2:9-10 ESV

Again we see the emphasis here on the special attention a woman should pay to the inner person of the heart, a heart surrendered to God which results in good works. Yet, this passage goes a step further and connects both the inner person and the outward appearance. Women were created to exhibit the qualities of Jesus inwardly, and dress outwardly in a modest and respectful way. Biblical modesty can be described as bashfulness towards men. A modest woman doesn't dress in a way to call attention to her body. She doesn't seek to make men lust after her, because she loves God and wants to honor His Word.

When we dress in a way that causes men to lust after us, we inadvertently contribute to their sin. Please hear me when I say that I am not blaming women for men's reactions. They are responsible for controlling themselves and their thoughts. Yet, because men are very visual creatures, we must be aware of the part we play by dressing immodestly. As our love for God and others grows, so should our sensitivity to causing others to sin.

"But I say to you that everyone who looks at a woman with lustful intent has already committed adultery with her in his heart." Matthew 5:28 ESV

There are two main factors which I believe contribute to our lack of modesty. The first is culture. As immorality increases in our culture, our standard of dress follows right along. Outfits that women would never dream of wearing in the 1950's are the norm now. Clothing gets smaller and smaller. Celebrities flaunt their bodies wearing barely-there outfits. Half-naked women abound on social media. As generation after generation of women are subjected to these images from a very early age they begin to view this as the norm and then follow suit, hoping to achieve beauty by the world's standards. We don't even realize how far we have strayed from the biblical concept of modesty, because instead of looking to God's Word to define what is appropriate and what isn't, we measure ourselves against the rest of society.

The second, which has been my personal experience as well, is women who dress immodestly looking for attention and affirmation from men. This was how I spent much of my life before God took hold of my heart. I looked to my image to affirm my worth. Truthfully, I wanted men to lust after me. Looking and feeling sexy gave me confidence, and that usually involved wearing clothes that left little to the imagination. I craved the approval of others, especially men. I'm sure this stemmed from my own father's absence in my life.

It was only once I felt the true love of my Heavenly Father that I began to stop looking for that love from everyone else. As my love for God grew, my desire to please Him also grew. The way I dressed changed and my desire to draw attention to myself also changed. I began to value God's opinion above all else. God values modesty so I now value modesty. The way I dress is an outward expression of my faith in Christ.

So as to walk in a manner worthy of the Lord, fully pleasing to Him, bearing fruit in every good work and increasing in the knowledge of God. Colossians 1:10 ESV

We can still dress fashionably and have our own unique sense of style without being immodest. We don't need to conform to the culture or draw attention to our bodies to please men, because we were created to please Jesus. Our bodies were bought with a price. He sees us as valuable because of who we have been uniquely designed to be, not because of how we look.

As we grow into all God created us to be, may the way we present ourselves reflect His purity. May the truths of His Word penetrate our souls and transform us from the inside out, as we strengthen our inner spirits to be beautiful and precious in God's eyes. His approval is the only approval we will ever need.

For am I now seeking the approval of man, or of God? Or am I trying to please man? If I were still trying to please man, I would not be a servant of Christ. Galatians 1:10 ESV

Personal Reflection:

Do I tend to put more focus on physical beauty or the beauty of my inner self? What steps can I take to make spiritual growth more of a priority?

Would I consider myself to have a gentle and quiet spirit? Why or why not? What changes need to be made in this area?

Do I dress modestly or do I dress in a way that causes men to lust after me? How can I view myself differently today and begin to honor God with the way I dress?

Heavenly Father, we praise Your name and thank You for Your timeless Word. Thank You for creating us to live in close relationship with You, relationship marked by faith, love, and obedience. We are so grateful that we can look to You to define beauty, rather than looking to the world around us. Help us to cultivate the inner beauty of a gentle and quiet spirit which is precious in Your eyes. Show us how to apply what we have learned today to our lives. Help us to prioritize our spiritual lives and seek to please You and You alone. Grow our faith into a faith that is confident and secure in Your love. Keep us humble and meek, like Jesus. Others-centered. Help us to reflect Your purity in all that we say, do, and wear. For those who look to men for approval and acceptance, we pray that You will speak to their souls today. That they will know how valued they are as Your daughters, and how much You love them. Thank You for giving each and every one of us worth, value, and purpose. In Jesus majestic and holy name, Amen.

Chapter 25
Created to be Calm

It is better to live on a corner of the housetop than in a house shared with a quarrelsome wife. Proverbs 21:9 ESV

Picture this man, shivering in the cold, perched on the corner of the roof. Gusts of wind hit him at high speed and threaten to catapult him to the ground below. Perhaps it is snowing, or thunder storming. Seems like this man would be pretty miserable, would you agree? Well, God's word says it is *worse* for this man to live in a house with a quarrelsome wife than to be on this roof. Although the image conjured up can be slightly comical, there is nothing funny about the deeper issue that lies within the woman who argues constantly.

Typically a quarrel is over a small issue and often ends up becoming a heated, angry argument. A quarrelsome wife is one who constantly flies off the handle and loses her temper. This wife is quick to argue and has a hard time keeping her emotions in check. She would be the exact opposite of the gentle and calm woman God designed each and every one of us to be.

Know this, my beloved brothers: let every person be quick to hear, slow to speak, slow to anger; for the anger of man does not produce the righteousness of God. Therefore put away all filthiness and rampant wickedness and receive with meekness the implanted word, which is able to save your souls.
James 1:19-21 ESV

In this passage, James equates anger with wickedness. He tells us to counter that wickedness by receiving God's Word with meekness, which we already learned is strength under control. In this way, our souls will be saved. This concept takes a bit of deeper explanation to grasp.

We are made up of three parts: body, spirit, and soul. Our spirit is the part of us that relates to God. Once we make Jesus our Lord and Savior, the Holy Spirit takes up residence inside our spirits. We are then saved and sealed for the day of redemption. Yet, our souls still need constant saving. The soul is comprised of the mind, will, and emotions. As we continually subject ourselves to God's Word, receiving it with meekness, our mind, will, and emotions will be kept pure and aligned with God's will. As we intentionally deal with our sin, in this case anger, our souls are renewed and God is glorified through our lives.

So what effects does anger have on us and how exactly do we put it away? Many believers, self- included, struggle with anger. Christian counselors report that over 50% of their patients wrestle with anger. An awareness of the consequences of anger is the first step to ridding ourselves of this toxic emotion.

The first effect of anger, and the most obvious, is that anger escalates conflict. Getting angry doesn't usually stop an argument; rather it fans the flames of that argument into an even bigger fire. This leads to more fighting and more anger. It is a vicious cycle. Hurtful words are spoken that can never be taken back. Relationships become strained, sometimes broken beyond repair. On the flip side, when we choose instead to respond gently, humbly, and in a Christ-like manner, conflict dissipates.

A soft answer turns away wrath, but a harsh word stirs up anger. Proverbs 15:1 ESV

A hot tempered man stirs up strife but he who is slow to anger quiets contention. Proverbs 15:18 ESV

Another consequence of anger is the grieving of the Holy Spirit. As believers, God's Spirit takes up permanent residence inside our bodies. The choices we make either bring Him joy or they cause Him to grieve. Because we are the Holy Spirit's dwelling place, He remains with us wherever we go. He gets an invite to every argument we attend. Since God hates sin, the Holy Spirit in us is also sensitive to sin. We bring Him much sorrow when we argue and allow anger to fester in our hearts.

Sometimes, rather than attacking others with angry words, we stuff our anger deep down inside. We refuse to deal with it in a healthy manner by cooperating with God to expose the root of the problem. This also grieves the Spirit, for stuffed anger will always explode at some point in the future. Stuffed anger also leads to bitterness and lack of forgiveness, both of which are contrary to the will of God.

And do not grieve the Holy Spirit of God by whom you were sealed for the day of redemption. Let all bitterness and wrath and anger and clamor and slander be put away from you, along with all malice. Ephesians 4:30-31 ESV

And the final consequence of anger is that we invite demonic presence into our lives. Sin lets the devil in. It's important to note the type of anger that does this, however. Not all anger is sinful. There are two times, biblically speaking, when anger isn't considered a sin. The first is when anger is dealt with appropriately, rather than spewing it out or suppressing it. It is not a sin to *be* angry. We all have emotions that will pop up whether we want them to or not. It's what we do with that anger that matters. I will discuss appropriate ways to deal with anger at the end of this chapter.

The second type of non-sinful anger is righteous anger. Righteous anger is what prompted Jesus to flip the tables of the money-changers in the temple. Jesus was angry at the way those men had blasphemed the house of God by using it as an opportunity to cheat people. His anger moved Him to action. This righteous anger also bubbled up in Paul when his spirit was provoked by all of the idol worship in Athens. This compelled Paul to debate daily with the people there, in order to make the true God known. In the same way, God infuses us with the anger that should motivate us to fight for justice and stand up for what is right. Righteous anger says – "I'm mad about this, and I'm going to channel this anger in a positive way to do something about it."

The type of anger that invites the devil into our lives is the anger that lies unchecked and unrepented of. This anger lurks beneath the surface just waiting to seep out. One act of anger after another and before long, it has become a pattern. Satan will use anger to gain ground in our lives and influence our behavior. The more we give in to anger, and refuse to repent and seek God's help to squash it, the more the enemy will be given the opportunity to affect us. Satan loves to torment believers. He delights in making us miserable, and finds great joy when he can tempt us to sin. We must be vigilant. We must stand firm and allow him no access to our lives.

Be angry and do not sin; do not let the sun go down on your anger, and give no opportunity to the devil.
Ephesians 4:26-27 ESV

I didn't realize I had anger problems until I had a teenager and a toddler at the same time. I thought it was just the frustrations of parenting that had turned me into an angry mom, but the truth is; that anger was there all along. It just took this particularly difficult season of life to bring it out of me. What is inside of us will always come out when we are bumped up against. Rather than blaming everyone else, I knew I had to face my own problem and get to the root of my anger. Thankfully, with Jesus, hope is never lost.

Just as gold is refined by fire, bringing the impurities to the surface to be scraped away, God uses the hard places in our lives to reveal the sin in our hearts so we can partner with Him to eradicate that sin from our lives.

But He knows the way that I take; when He has tried me, I shall come out as gold. Job 23:10 ESV

This can be a long process. I still struggle with my anger at times. Yet, the quicker I am to repent and seek God's forgiveness when I lose my temper, the less hold anger will have on my soul. God will continue to use trials to refine me into the woman He created me to be. He will use the difficulties in all of our lives to shape us into the image of Christ.

Once the sin of our hearts is exposed we see where our weaknesses lie, which gives God's power the chance to truly shine. After gold is refined it is typically too soft to be of any use on its own, so other metals must be added so it can reach its maximum potential. In the same way, as God brings our impurities to the surface we must acknowledge that we are not strong enough to tackle them in our own strength. We must rely on the power of the Holy Spirit to overcome deep-seated anger issues. While there are practical steps we can take to manage our anger, there are some things only God can do.

Search me, O God, and know my heart! Try me and know my thoughts! And see if there be any grievous way in me, and lead me in the way everlasting! Psalm 139:23-24 ESV

So what are some practical steps we can take in the heat of the moment when we feel anger boiling up inside of us, threatening to come out in an unhealthy way? How should we react when we are being provoked or treated unfairly? Well, we have no better model to look to than Jesus Himself. He was oppressed, afflicted, beaten and bruised, spit upon, and taunted, yet He did not open His mouth against his tormentors. He refused to lash out at them in anger. Instead, He loved these people and asked the Father to forgive them. In this same manner, when others provoke our anger we should respond in love.

Do not be overcome by evil, but overcome evil with good.
Romans 12:21 ESV

It sounds so cliché, but stopping to breathe and count to ten really helps in these types of situations. Pausing before responding in anger gives us a chance to recall specific Scriptures and remind ourselves to honor God with our reactions. I've also found it helpful to ask whoever is provoking me to an argument to give me some space so I can calm down before I yell or say something hurtful. I can tell when I'm getting worked up and just need a little time to think and relax. Many times this can be exactly we need to keep our tempers in check and avoid acting in a way we will later regret. During this time we can pray and seek God's wisdom on how to move forward.

The heart of the righteous ponders how to answer.
Proverbs 15:29a ESV

Identifying the triggers that cause our anger to erupt is also key. Often, anger issues stem from past experiences, and possibly childhood trauma that was never dealt with. I realized over the course of dealing with my own anger that mine stems from my desire for control. When I feel like I'm not in control of a situation, or people aren't doing what I want them to do, it sparks my anger. Sometimes counseling is needed to unearth the reasons we act the way we do. We can rest assured that, wherever this anger stems from, God wants to heal and restore us. He never exposes our sin to condemn us. He exposes our sin so we can work together with Him to remove it and grow into the women we were designed to be.

We can take comfort in knowing that as we partner with God to eradicate anger from our lives, our faith will grow exponentially. The bond we have with our Heavenly Father will be strengthened in the most amazing way. He will work miracles in our hearts, and when He does, our lives will also change. When difficult people and trying circumstances come our way, it will be a cause to rejoice because we will know God is at work in our souls!

Count it all joy, my brothers, when you meet trials of various kinds, for you know that the testing of your faith produces steadfastness. And let steadfastness have its full effect, that you may be perfect and complete, lacking in nothing.
James 1:2-4 ESV

Personal Reflection:
Would I consider myself a quarrelsome person? Do I argue with my loved ones often? Do I value being right more than I value my relationships?

Would others say that I have a temper and fly off the handle easily? Can I identify the triggers and possible roots of my anger?

Have I allowed bitterness and anger to reign in my heart? If so, what steps can I take to put my anger away?

Heavenly Father, thank You for Your amazing Word which shines its light into our hearts and brings about restoration and healing. We want to honor You with every choice we make, and that includes how we react when others upset us. Give us the wisdom to seek You when we begin to get angry. Help us to remember specific Scriptures that we can use as guides for dealing with anger. Help us to be slow to speak, quick to listen, and slow to anger. Forgive us for the times we have not dealt with anger in the appropriate way. Forgive us for the times we have grieved Your precious Holy Spirit. Keep us sensitive to the sin of anger and the effect it has on You and others. Help us to be peacemakers who use soft words. Give us spirits of gentleness and self control. We pray that any doors we have opened to the enemy will be shut as we repent of our anger and turn to You, surrendering all and asking for Your guidance. Let the devil have no foothold in our lives. Thank You for refining us through our trials to look more and more like Jesus. Help us to always seek out the lessons You are teaching us through our difficult seasons. We rejoice that we are Your daughters! In Jesus mighty and beautiful name, Amen.

Chapter 26
Created to Trust God

"Blessed is she who has believed that the Lord would fulfill his promises to her!" Luke 1:45 NIV

Belief: Confident trust, dependency, and reliance upon someone or something.

Believe. It seems so simple and straightforward, yet this is often where we struggle the most. We were created to be women who would possess such a confident certainty in, and dependence on, our Heavenly Father that nothing would ever shake us. Trust begins with knowing God's character. God deserves every ounce of our trust.

He is the Maker of all things, the Sovereign Ruler of this universe and the Giver of everything good. He cannot lie. He is a covenant-keeping God and his promises remain true until the end of time. If God said it, He will do it. He is omnipresent (everywhere at once), omnipotent (has unlimited power), and omniscience (knows everything). It is on these truths that we can confidently rest our hopes. No matter what circumstances may look like, God is in full control. We can trust Him.

Great is our Lord and abundant in power; His understanding is beyond measure. Psalm 147:5 ESV

Becoming acquainted with God's character is key to trusting Him. Consider Mary, the mother of our precious Lord Jesus. Think of the many emotions and thoughts that must have buzzed through her head when the angel told her she would miraculously conceive and give birth to the long-awaited Savior! I imagine she thought, "Was this really happening? Would God actually fulfill this promise? How would this look to Joseph, who she was betrothed to marry?"

Despite her fear, and the many questions she must have asked herself, she was familiar with the character of God. She knew He could be trusted to fulfill His Word. She could also depend on Him to figure out the details and walk her through this incredible journey. He would be with her every step of the way. She knew God. She believed God. In turn, she was blessed by God.

And Mary said, "My soul magnifies the Lord, and my spirit rejoices in God my Savior, for He has looked on the humble estate of his servant. For behold, from now on all generations will call me blessed; for He who is mighty has done great things for me, and holy is His name." Luke 1:45-49 ESV

Along with Mary, we find many people in the Bible who trusted God completely. Noah constructed the ark when there was not even a hint of rain. Abraham followed God into a great and unknown land, with only a promise to guide him. David trusted that the Lord would go before him in battle when he couldn't foresee the outcome. The centurion was confident that Jesus just had to say the word for his daughter to be healed. The woman with internal bleeding knew if she could only touch the hem of Jesus' garment, she would be well.

On the flip side of this, there are many times Jesus had to admonish people for their lack of belief. When a storm raged around the boat that held them, the disciples feared for their lives and frantically woke the sleeping Jesus. The disciples worried that the storm would overtake their boat and plunge them into the sea.

They forgot who stood beside them. Jesus commanded the waves of the sea to cease, and rebuked the disciples for their lack of faith.

We see this unbelief again when a father doubted whether Jesus could cast a demon out of his son. Part of the man believed, yet part of him still doubted. Jesus reminded the man that all things are possible to those who believe. To this the man responded, "I believe; help my unbelief!" (Mark 9:24) Sometimes this needs to be our prayer as well! Belief is a prerequisite for receiving God's amazing promises. We must believe He is who He says He and will do what He said He will do.

And without faith it is impossible to please Him, for whoever would draw near to God must believe that He exists and that He rewards those who seek Him. Hebrews 11:6 ESV

Our faith solidifies as our relationship with God grows. As I look back over the years I have walked with Him, I can recall countless times He has proved Himself faithful. I've experienced Him to be exactly who He says He is in the Bible, and have seen His promises fulfilled in my life and the lives of my loved ones. It is so amazing! My faith started out so small, yet has now blossomed into something big and beautiful. I know I can place absolute trust in my Heavenly Father. I am confident that His Word never fails.

If you aren't at this place yet in your relationship with God, that's ok! We all have a starting point. Faith like this doesn't come automatically, it is a process. Your trust in God will build as you continually seek Him and step out in faith when He asks you to. You were created to hear Him, know Him, and believe Him. He is worthy of your trust.

And those who know your name put their trust in you, for
you, O Lord, have not forsaken those who seek you.
Psalm 9:10 ESV

God always keeps His promises. If He promises something in His Word, it will come to pass. When studying God's promises throughout Scripture, we must be able to differentiate between which promises are for us and which promises only applied to others. Although God may use any Scripture to encourage us, rebuke us, or train us in righteousness, there are certain promises that were only made to specific people at a specific time.

For instance, in the Old Testament, God sometimes promised wealth for obedience. Those promises were strictly for the Israelites living in those time periods. They do not apply to us today. Obedience brings many blessings, and God does promise to provide and supply our needs, but we are not promised riches and financial prosperity.

We also must be able to distinguish between unconditional and conditional promises. There are many unconditional promises for believers in Scripture, which means they don't require action on our part for fulfillment. Here are a few examples of these:

God will supply the needs of believers.

And my God will supply every need of yours according to His
riches in glory in Christ Jesus. Philippians 4:19 ESV

A true believer's salvation is eternally secure.

"My sheep hear my voice, and I know them, and they follow
me. I give them eternal life, and they will never perish, and no
one will snatch them out of my hand." John 10:28-29 ESV

Nothing can separate a believer from God's love.

For I am sure that neither death nor life, nor angels nor rulers, nor things present nor things to come, nor powers, nor height nor depth, nor anything else in all creation, will be able to separate us from the love of God in Christ Jesus our Lord. Romans 8:37-38 ESV

If we are believers in Christ these promises are ours to stand on, along with many, many more. In addition, we have conditional promises. These promises are usually centered around obedience. We can also call these if/then promises. Here are a few:

If we trust God and put Him first, He will straighten our paths.

Trust in the Lord with all your heart, and do not lean on your own understanding. In all your ways acknowledge Him, and He will make straight your paths. Proverbs 3:5-6 ESV

If we confess our sins, God forgives and refreshes us.

If we confess our sins, He is faithful and just to forgive us our sins and to cleanse us from all unrighteousness. 1 John 1:9 ESV

If we keep our eyes on Jesus then we will have peace.

You keep him in perfect peace whose mind is stayed on you. Isaiah 26:3 ESV

Memorizing and praying God's promises keeps us centered on Him and fosters a strong faith. This is especially beneficial when the circumstances of our lives do not at all line up with what we know God has spoken. For instance, we know God works all things for good in the lives of those who love Him (Romans 8:28). Still, there are times when we look around us and we see nothing good. We wonder how God can possibly be at work in the midst of our struggles. This is where faith enters in.

Faith is bigger than what we can see with our natural eyes. Faith rests confidently in God's promises, regardless if we understand why things are happening the way they are. God's promises usually don't happen on our timetable, but we must trust that His timing is perfect. Just because He is silent, does not mean He is absent. Our prayers are not hitting the ceiling. He hears us. He loves us. He goes ever before us.

You go before me and follow me. You place your hand of blessing on my head. Psalm 139:5 NLT

Because God sees all and knows all, we can trust that His promises will come to pass exactly when they are supposed to. We may not understand why things happen the way they do in our lives, but we can trust that God always has a purpose. Often times, He develops characteristics in us that never would have been there had we not gone through this trial, or that disappointment. He strengthens our dependence on Him during the valley moments and uses them to build our faith and trust in Him. We can be confident that He has everything worked out, for our good and for His glory.

How precious is your steadfast love, O God! The children of mankind take refuge in the shadow of your wings. Psalm 36:7 ESV

There is no safer place to be than resting in God's shadow. To rest in His shadow is to be close to Him. To follow Him wherever He leads. This kind of intimacy comes from putting Jesus first and seeking Him with all of our hearts. Giving Him our full trust. Stepping out in faith when He asks us to and watching as He shows up. We were designed to be women who would stand firm in every season. May we hold fast to this truth: the very same God who put the stars into place is the One who holds our lives in His hands!

He who dwells in the shelter of the Most High will abide in the shadow of the Almighty. I will say to the Lord, "My refuge and my fortress, my God in whom I trust." Psalm 91:1-2 ESV

Personal Reflection:
Do I truly believe that God is for me and not against me? Do I trust His character and believe His promises are true? Why or why not?

Have I allowed unanswered prayers or unfulfilled promises to weaken my faith? If this has affected my intimacy with God what steps can I take to make strengthen my faith?

Are there specific promises I need to hold on to during this season of my life?

Heavenly Father, we praise You for Your trustworthy character. We thank You for always being dependable. You are a God who keeps Your promises! Thank You for all of the amazing promises in Your word for those who believe and trust in the name of Jesus. We don't deserve Your goodness, yet You continually overflow with mercy and love towards us. We know that we can trust every word that proceeds from Your mouth. Thank You for your faithfulness. Please strengthen our faith in times of trial. Help us to stand on Your promises, even when we aren't seeing them manifest in our lives on our time schedule. Help us to look for the lessons You are teaching us in the waiting. Remind us that You continually work all things for our good, no matter what circumstances might say. Help our unbelief! Give us the strength and wisdom needed to sustain us through the difficult seasons. Remind us that You go before us. Keep us close to You and abiding in the love of Jesus. We pray for those who have lost faith in You. Father, we ask that You would remind them of Your trustworthy nature. We pray You would show up in their lives in a mighty way. You see the big picture, and even when things don't make sense to us, they always do to You. Your ways are higher than our own. May we rest today and all days, in the shadow of Your Almighty wings. In Jesus precious name, Amen.

Chapter 27
Created to Find our Identity in Christ

God is in the midst of her, she shall not be moved.
Psalm 46:5a ESV

This Scripture belongs to a beautiful Psalm written by the sons of Korah. This Psalm, referred to by Charles Spurgeon as the song of holy confidence, recounts the mighty works of the Lord, and the amazing wonders He has performed. This all-powerful God, who rules the universe and is sovereign over all, is the same God who strengthens and protects His people. He is our refuge, our fortress. The "she" referred to in this passage is the city of God (cities in the Bible were often referred to with female pronouns). The Lord dwelt within the midst of this city.

The Hebrew word used here for midst was *qereb,* a word that meant the center of something. When this word was used in reference to a person it signified the inner being, the innermost self. Because God was at the center of this city, it would never be moved. Other Bible translations say it would not fall, or couldn't be destroyed. Wherever God dwells will be as fortified as this city. Unshakeable. Impenetrable.

Because God's very Spirit dwells in *us*, we, like this city God inhabits, will never be moved. God is for us and not against us. He has chosen us, adopted us into His family, and given us new identities. He inhabits the center of our innermost beings.

For all who are led by the Spirit of God are sons of God.
Romans 8:14 ESV

What exactly does this change of identity entail? What is different now that God's Spirit abides in us? We are brand new women now. The old has passed away and the new has come. We are God's redeemed daughters, blessed beyond measure. We are heirs of God and fellow heirs with Christ. We can claim God's promises, presence, and power as our inheritance. We have a new purpose in life, a new hope, and a new mission. God has bestowed upon us a new name.

God changed the names of specific people in the Bible to signify their new destiny and establish their fresh identity as His people. Abram's name was changed to Abraham and his wife Sarai's name to Sarah. God had altered their destiny in a miraculous way and the name change would be a permanent reminder of His faithfulness. Jacob's name was changed to Israel. This would establish His new identity as one who had overcome. By this change, Jacob gained the strength he needed to put his scandalous past behind him and grow into the man God had created him to be.

Jesus changed Simon's name to Peter. He declared that Peter would be the rock on which the church was built. Peter went from being an arrogant and impulsive man to a strong and bold leader of the early church. Saul's name was changed to Paul when God radically changed his life, in one of the most amazing transformations in Scripture. Paul went from being a hostile persecutor of Christians to a man who would spread the gospel near and far, and write a large chunk of the New Testament.

In the same way that God bestowed new names upon these men, He wants to give us new names as well. He doesn't do this in a literal way, but in the sense of embracing our new identity as Christ-followers. He wants us to leave the past behind and step into our destiny as His daughters. To walk in the fullness of everything we have been designed to be.

"Remember not the former things, nor consider the things of old. Behold, I am doing a new thing; now it springs forth, do you not perceive it?" Isaiah 43:18-19a ESV

When we allow the truth of who we are in Christ to make its home deep down in our souls, it will cultivate in us the confidence to trust God entirely and follow wherever He leads. When we arm ourselves with the truth of who we are, we will stand strong against the lies of culture, critics, and the enemy. We are not who *they* say we are. We are who *God* says we are.

We are children of God.

But to all who did receive Him, who believed in His name, He gave the right to become children of God. John 1:12 ESV

We have peace with God.

Therefore, since we have been justified by faith, we have peace with God through our Lord Jesus Christ. Romans 5:1 ESV

God helps us.

Let us then with confidence draw near to the throne of grace, that we may receive mercy and find grace to help in time of need. Hebrews 4:16 ESV

We are tenderly loved by God.

I have loved you with an everlasting love; I have drawn you with unfailing kindness. Jeremiah 31:3 NIV

We are temples in which God dwells.

Do you not know that you are God's temple and that God's Spirit dwells in you? 1 Corinthians 3:16 ESV

We are Christ's friends.

"No longer do I call you servants, for the servant does not know what his master is doing; but I have called you friends, for all that I have heard from my Father I have made known to you." John 15:15 ESV

We are united to God, in one spirit.

But he who is joined to the Lord becomes one spirit with Him. 1 Corinthians 6:17 ESV

We are chosen by God to be built up in Christ.

As you come to Him, a living stone rejected by men but in the sight of God chosen and precious, you yourselves like living stones are being built up as a spiritual house, to be a holy priesthood, to offer spiritual sacrifices acceptable to God through Jesus Christ. 1 Peter 2:5 ESV

We may approach God with confidence and boldness.

{Christ Jesus} in whom we have boldness and access with confidence through our faith in Him. Ephesians 3:12 ESV

We are God's coworkers.

For we are God's fellow workers. You are God's field, God's building. 1 Corinthians 3:9 ESV

We have direct access to God and are part of His family.

For through Him we both have access in one Spirit to the Father. So then you are no longer strangers and aliens, but you are fellow citizens with the saints and members of the household of God. Ephesians 2:18-19 ESV

We are holy and blameless before God.

Even as he chose us in Him before the foundation of the world, that we should be holy and blameless before Him. Ephesians 1:4 ESV

God is working all things for our good.

And we know that for those who love God all things work together for good, for those who are called according to His purpose. Romans 8:28 ESV

We have been established, anointed, and sealed by God.

And it is God who establishes us with you in Christ, and has anointed us, and who has also put His seal on us and given us His Spirit in our hearts as a guarantee. 2 Corinthians 1:21-22 ESV

God will finish what He started in us.

And I am sure of this, that He who began a good work in you will bring it to completion at the day of Jesus Christ. Philippians 1:6 ESV

We are citizens of heaven.

But our citizenship is in heaven, and from it we await a Savior, the Lord Jesus Christ. Philippians 3:20 ESV

God strengthens us for everything.

I can do all things through Him who strengthens me. Philippians 4:13 ESV

This is not nearly a complete list of all of the truths that are now applicable to your life because you are a follower of Jesus. I encourage you to explore your Bible for even more. Memorize them, post them around your house, be sure to think about them daily. Know who God says you are and remind yourself often of your identity in Christ. Let these Scriptures carry you through the ups and downs of life until the day comes when you meet Jesus face to face. Have your mind, heart, and soul so full of God's truths that there won't be any room at all for the devil's lies!!

Put on the whole armor of God that you may be able to stand against the schemes of the devil. Ephesians 6:11 ESV

****

Friends, it has been such an amazing journey together through God's Word! My prayer for you is that, by this time, you have a firm grasp on who God is and exactly what kind of woman He designed you to be. I hope you feel equipped to live a life that honors your Creator, a life that will be lived right in the center of His will.

My prayer is that through this process you have drawn closer to your Heavenly Father, and allowed His truths to transform your soul. My desire is for peace, joy, and love to abound in your heart. I pray you are growing stronger day by day in your faith and, empowered by the Holy Spirit, walking in obedience to all that the Lord asks of you. Above all, I hope you are delighting in your relationship with Jesus, and excited about the future of your journey with Him. I pray you are becoming a woman who lives her life with passion and purpose. For this, my precious friend, is exactly the woman you were created to be!

For this reason I kneel before the Father, from whom every family in heaven and on earth derives its name. I pray that out of his glorious riches He may strengthen you with power through His Spirit in your inner being, so that Christ may dwell in your hearts through faith. And I pray that you, being rooted and established in love, may have power, together with all the Lord's holy people, to grasp how wide and long and high and deep is the love of Christ, and to know this love that surpasses knowledge – that you may be filled to the measure of all the fullness of God. Now to Him who is able to do far more abundantly than all that we ask or think, according to the power at work within us, to Him be glory in the church and in Christ Jesus throughout all generations, forever and ever. Amen. Ephesians 3:14-19 ESV

****

Notes

Author's Contact Information

Amy Duggins

Website: Honorgodmindbodysoul.com

Email: amyduggins@honorgodmindbodysoul.com

Facebook: Amy Duggins

Made in the USA
Coppell, TX
28 September 2023

22151080R00118